Tales of Kumander Misis ang Wifey ni Tsip (Tales of Commander Mrs.)

Cherry Moriones Doromal

Published by Cherry Moriones Doromal, 2018.

TALES OF KUMANDER MISIS ANG WIFEY NI TSIP (TALES OF COMMANDER MRS.)

First edition. May 11, 2018.

ISBN: 979-8231289479

Written by Cherry Moriones Doromal.

Tales of Kumander Misis, Ang Wifey ni Tsip

Published by Cherry Doromal at Smashwords

Smashwords Edition

ACKNOWLEDGEMENTS

First of all, let me clarify that this is very much a vital part of this book. In my heart, "Acknowledgement" is my Page One, Chapter One.

Top on my list is our Heavenly Father who deserves all praises and honor for all His mighty works in my life from my conception till today, to eternity.

I would like to recognize, as well, my dearest family, and friends who stick closer than real brothers and sisters to me, for all their unwavering encouragement, trust and support in all of my endeavors.

Special credit to Mr. Argel Penasbo for the art work on my cover, and my son Zekie for his kind help in my formatting. Many thanks, of course, to Strong for charging my gadgets and bringing awakening snacks to me as I write.

To all my friends and followers in blogs and social media, you are such an inspiration. Without your energizing personal messages, greetings, likes and comments, this project, as well as those in progress and those to come soon will not ever materialize.

This humble work is lovingly dedicated to all of you who I am truly grateful to.

For some time, I had almost forgotten that I should come up with hardcopy and ebook versions of Tales of Kumander Misis since the social media version has been doing well and is easy to manage. The circumstances, though, have organized themselves to compel me to publish this book... How magnificent it is that everything else progressed in favor of me to finally see this work in bookshelves.

For that reason, as much as I want to share my own long quotes, I opt to share this verse instead, as it encompasses what I wanted to say to all our readers:

"Commit your work to the LORD, and your plans will be established." Proverbs 16:3

Enjoy reading!

Sincerely,

Cherry Moriones- Doromal
Author

Meet Kumander Misis

More than a plain police officer's wife, Cherry Moriones-Doromal is an integrated marketing communications professional with twenty-four years of combined management exposure and experience in local and international public relations, quad-media (radio-tv-print-online), marketing, publication, and advertising. She is also a musical composer, professional writer and editor. Among other prestigious business and scholarly titles, she previously assumed the positions of Editor of the Manila Bulletin Online —the oldest and well-esteemed newspaper in the Philippines, CEO of Earthwide Concepts Inc. of Las Vegas NV, Editor-In-Chief of the broadsheet The Phil Am Press of Daly City and Southern CA and had held various stints as managing director of reputable marketing and advertising companies.

Cherry is currently a columnist and entertainment editor of Republiq Magazine of Southern CA, USA. During her free time, she goes to her home kitchen to make artisan products called "The Green Kitchen" gourmet products which she promotes online and distributed nationwide through Purple Kitchen Marketing Company which she owns.

As of this writing, aside from being a licensed educator specializing in English and Literature, with International Baccalaureate (IB), International Primary Curriculum (IPC), International General Certificate of Secondary Education (IGCSE), Multiple Intelligences (MI) and K-12 trainings, Cherry is also a doting mom to two brilliant sons who are both academic scholars at a prominent international school.

In college, as one of the few scholars of the City of Manila, Cherry had undergone almost two years of AB Psychology studies before she finished Bachelor of Mass Communication at the Pamantasan ng Lungsod ng Maynila (PLM) or University of the City of Manila. As a duly elected student leader, she thrivingly represented the City in numerous local and international conferences. The author who is a lifelong learner also finished Bachelor of Laws and Master in Business Administration, and is pursuing Master of Educational Management.

Cherry's passion in all of her undertakings did not remain unnoticed. Thus, for her years of active community leadership, ecclesiastical work, volunteerism, and social entrepreneurship, Cherry received various awards and recognitions from the local government, The Office of the President, the Philippine National Police, and NGOs. She was also granted an honorary degree Doctorate of Strategic Missions at International Communicators Open University by Evangelical Bishops in the University of the Philippines.

About Tsip

Police Supt. Wilson Layag Doromal labeled as "Darling of the Press" by media friends in the Philippines is a graduate of Class '98 of the Philippine National Police Academy. Prior to his training at PNPA, he finished Bachelor of Business Administration at the Lyceum of the Philippines where he was an active ROTC Officer. He finished his MBA in 2002.

Back in College, Wilson was technically a working scholar as he co-administered his family's security agency business alongside his schooling. Being born of and raised by a Philippine Constabulary Officer Lt. Col. Nelson Del Corro Doromal and a loving mother Aida Layag Doromal, he grew up with strong familiarity, indisputable reverence and solid passion to the military and police service.

Aside from top gun, marksmanship and sharpshooter recognitions and various commendations and leadership awards, among his trainings are Explosive Ordnance Disposal (EOD), Anti- Terrorist Investigation Course (USA), Terrorist Devices Threat and Response Course, Underwater Demolition Course, Underwater Ordnance Disposal Training, Tactical Explosive Breeching Training, SCUBA Dive Supervisor Course, Executive Motorcycle Riding Course, VIP Security , Criminal Investigation and Detective Management Course, Advance Finance Course and many others.

On September 2017, Col. Doromal left his position as Deputy Chief of Police for Administration (DCOPA) of Paranaque City to give way to professional advancement where he had taken the Public Safety Officers Senior Executive Course. The year after, upon culmination of said course, he received an academic recognition from National Police College for obtaining the highest grade of 96.2% in Team Action Research, entitled "Investigative Capability of Criminal

Investigation and Detection Group in CALABARZON in Preventing and Countering Violent Extremism."

Col. Doromal also held various positions at the Manila Police District, such as Station Commander of Station 11 (Chinatown), Station Commander of Station 10 (Pandacan), Police Community Precinct Commander of Lawton-Cityhall, PCP Commander of Gagalangin Tondo, PCP Commander of Harbour Park (Port) and Chief of Operations of Station 1.

As junior officer, he was also assigned at the CIDG, DIDM and Region 4 (CALABARZON and MIMAROPA). He also held the post of Provincial Officer of HPG Laguna, Region 4A and Deputy Regional Chief of Highway Patrol Group in Region 3 (Bulacan, Pampanga, Zambales, Aurora, Nueva Ecija, Tarlac) and HPG Clearance Station Chief of Valenzuela, Caloocan, Muntinlupa, Pasay, and Las Pinas.

While he is a strong advocate of servant leadership, as in his language, "Service to people is service to God," Col. Wilson Doromal is known to be a constant and serious campaigner of community involvement in crime prevention and maintenance of peace and order. He always believes that attaining a zero-crime community or city is possible through multi-sectoral support and vigilance.

Over the years, he demonstrated credence in the supremacy of unity among different sectors of society as shown when he founded the GISPO (Gagalangin Integrated Sectors for Peace and Order) while he was Precinct Commander of Gagalangin, Manila Police District. Likewise, when he was the Precinct Commander of Lawton, Station 5 Manila, he founded the Ayala-Taft Anti-Crime Consortium, HPG Force Multiplier Inc. in Region 4 and PRO-ACTIV in Binondo-Chinatown, all of which had been dynamic partners of the local police in peace enforcement and successful capture of criminals.

Prologue

Hello! My name is Cherry—the one herein being referred to as *Kumander Misis, Ang Wifey ni Tsip,* or literally translated as *Commander Mrs., The Chief's Wife.* Whereas, the herein character Tsip is my spouse Col. Wilson Layag Doromal of the Philippine National Police.

Through this inspirational and partly humorous writing, I am exposing to the world my day-to-day life as a police officer's better half, with high hopes that my stories, struggles and victory founded through solid partnership with my husband and the Almighty would inspire the readers.

The first four chapters of the book cover Tsip and Kumander's unpublished love story prior to marriage. The rest of the chapters will provide you with wisdom-packed stories about their married and family life. I deemed it suitable, as well, to incorporate some updated versions, with behind-the-scene accounts of my previous blogs, discourses, compositions, and writings for a broader reach.

Now, why Kumander Misis? As it is being flippantly uttered in the military and police service, the wife is always one to two ranks higher than her husband. Do you agree? That remains debatable of course.

In this book, let me authenticate the veracity of that notion... at least in our own family. Therefore, allow me please to share with you the perks of having a *Kumander Misis* at home, for your guidance and consideration.

Without further ado, let me start gossiping big time about my life being a police officer's wife.

Remember: "Behind every man's success is a Kumander Misis."

The Author

CHAPTER ONE

Caught by the Irony

Prior to my marriage in 2000, I never envisaged myself getting married or having a family of my own. No one could ever imagine, I suppose, that I would soon be married to a police officer.

In all honesty, initially, I had no idea about what exactly a police does and what the police service is all about. But Heavens have better unforeseen plans for me.

How paradoxical it was that shortly after my marriage, I became one of the leaders of COPPS Inc. or Christian Officers of the Philippine Police Service, founded by some police generals such as Police Deputy Director General Enrique B. Galang and Police Director Reynold Osia who later on, invited me to become one of the directors of the National Council of Reformed Presbyterian Movement along with distinguished Korean bishops. COPPS, a Christian organization based in Camp Crame, was a steadfast advocate for the nationwide moral transformation of the Philippine National Police. With God's help, we had successfully sponsored various transformation programs at PNP in collaboration with local government units, non-governmental organizations, youth organizations and religious and business entities.

After some time, PECSVI or Peace Enforcers Citizens Scout Volunteers Inc. was born. Together with a greater number of supporters from COPPS led by Bishop Jesse Penoso and high-ranking police officials, we went around schools, barangays, cities and churches to implement anti-drug and volunteerism campaigns.

To further the irony, at present, I am actively involved, in my humblest way, in the nationwide multisectoral effort to transform the Philippine National Police through the Integrated Transformation Program- Performance Governance System (ITP-PGS), in my capacity as member of the District Advisory Council of the Southern Police District.

During my earliest media stints, on the radio news program Tinig ng Taong Bayan (Voice of the People) of DWOO 774khz anchored by the then veteran broadcaster James Brown Pagkatipunan, I remember how as a newbie reporter, I would always attack erring police officers in my news reports. We had segments like Modus Operandi and Huli Ka! (Caught You!) where through those segments, I would usually take joy and pride at lambasting police officers.

As I'm writing this part today, like a movie playing in my mind, I got to recall the segment teaser that I made for "Huli Ka!" segment which I'm sharing with you—for my archive— as follows:

"Nagtatago, pasilip-silip,
Dahah-dahan para hindi sumabit.
Patalikod na kinakalaban pamahalaan at mamamayan.
Hindi makapangloloko dahil huli sa akto.
Kahit sino ka pa, HULI KA!"

Translated for you as:

"Hiding and peeping,
Gently that they may not be trapped,
Attacking the government and people in silence,
Never can they trick us as they've been caught in the act
Whoever you are, we "Caught You!"

Come to think of it, as far as I know, I was among the first to conceptualize and incorporate satirical poetry in my news back in 1993 at the esteemed Mareco Broadcasting Network. The irony of ironies is that I was just so pleased at sharing undesirable reports about police personalities back then and would end up in aggressive statements similar to this in Tagalog:

"Corrupt Policeman, abuser of people,
Change your ways today before we kick you out of your post."

CHAPTER TWO

First Sight

It was in the 3rd quarter of 1999 that I first heard from an acquaintance the name of one Police Inspector Wilson who wanted to meet me in person. After several attempts, for whatever reason, our schedules wouldn't meet. Until the last quarter of 1999 came where we finally got to talk on phone, exchanged text messages and soon met up at TGI Friday's Robinson's Ermita when I was with my lawyer friends who were having a conference at the adjacent Manila Midtown Hotel.

Partiality aside, Wilson has a certain approachable personality that every person would love. He is naturally transparent and spontaneous, but never irritating. I think the reason is that he has no luggage of arrogance or insecurity in his system, and that he is naturally kindhearted. You will discover more about this in the coming chapters of the book.

Back to business, the scenario of our first meeting went like this:

Wilson to me on phone: *"So, you'll be at Fridays by 5PM? Since I'm here in Quezon City now, I would love to come and see you there at TGIF. By the way, for you to recognize me, I'll be in blue top."*

As you might have observed, the shade of blue Wilson was supposed to wear wasn't clear in our conversation. Furthermore, Wilson didn't mention the type of top he would wear — I had no idea if it was polo, t-shirt, barong, and all that. All he said was that he would be in blue top when he comes.

Around 5:15 pm (late by design!), I came to Fridays and saw just after the entrance, a greasy-headed man in his 50s, who was wearing a loose and dazzling bright blue floral Hawaiian polo. He was staring and smiling at me, as if he knew me and was in love with me, hahah. In my mind, I said: "Oh I'm dead!" I was horrendously thinking that he was the Wilson I had been talking to on phone all those days who, regrettably, was my date that night.

It's funny how I was resiliently and forcefully pushing myself to approach the table to greet the man. I was hesitant as I felt like an elastic band as I wanted to contract, to turn back or ran away upon reaching the "point of no return". Just in time when I was about to say hello to the stranger, I received a call from the real Wilson who said he was waiting for me for almost an hour beforehand, and that he was sitting at the bar on the other side of the restaurant.

At that point, in my mind I said: "*Oh thanks! (sigh, sigh, sigh) I hope that the real Wilson is an improved version!*"

To cut the story short, I waited for Wilson to approach me as I was seated on a separate table. Of course, I needed to play like a modern Maria Clara, as in prim and proper, since I knew that he's a police officer whose exposure could have been comparable to "The Fast and the Furious."

True enough, like the speed of light, right then and there during our very first meeting, the gentleman sat straight beside me, though in an endearing manner, without my permission. I never expected that he would pull his chair right next to me, with a distance of nearly one-inch away! In the language, his demeanors were surprisingly "astig" or cool, right?

We didn't stay long at TGIF that night as I needed to go home. Then, Mr. Police Inspector took me to our home for the first time.

CHAPTER THREE

Courtship, Police Style

At the time I met him, Police Inspector Wilson Doromal was the aide-de-camp of CIDG Director (who would later be our wedding principal sponsor) Gen. Lucas Managuelod. As aide-de-camp, he was with his boss everywhere the latter went. In sum, the young officer operated as the head of the general's security team, and acted as executive secretary, as well. Hence, Wilson's days and nights even on weekends were dedicated to his work.

Whereas in the eyes of the laymen, the job was prestigious, in reality, the entry-level officer's work was tantamount to a lowly G.P.A. or "Great Personal Assistant"— cellphone handler, human directory, instant call center, and the like. When the boss had to leave at 6:30 am from his home in Quezon City, Inspector Doromal and his team should be there one to two hours ahead.

After my first date with Inspector Doromal, the more that he would regularly call me, page me, and send me text messages to report his whereabouts every single day. Though I didn't know exactly why the young officer had to inform me of all his activities as we had no formal commitment with each other yet whatsoever, I remember feeling pleased that he was doing that.

In February 2000, from CIDG Camp Crame, Gen. Lucas Managuelod took with him Inspector Doromal at Camp Vicente Lim in Laguna when the general assumed the position of Regional Director of PRO 4. In other words, Laguna instantly became Wilson's new home.

At a normal glance, it was almost impossible for me and Inspector Wilson to find time for a serious romantic relationship. In those times, just imagine how hectic my itinerary was, as well, that I had to multitask.

I was running my advertising company located in Panay Avenue with extension office in Greenhills, while concurrently hosting television shows "Business Zone" and "Talking Heads" at Zoe Broadcasting Network (TV 11 at that time). On the side, I was law schooling at PLM, and leading various university-wide student activities in my capacity as President of the Supreme Student Council of the Pamantasan ng Lungsod ng Maynila. It was also the period where I would be frequently sent by the city to various conferences locally and internationally within my term. Other than those, I also had active suitors who had been there for years and who would take time guarding me during the day even to my night classes, to the point of invading our law library. These gentlemen—one, two or three of them—would wait for me in the library till our dismissal time. Whewww, blame it on my long hair!

The Normal Abnormality.

So, where or how did Inspector Doromal get my attention?

Wilson never showed any form of insecurity or ruthlessness whenever I had other suitors around. He would confidently and amicably talk even to my most devoted suitors. I remember one time how in the presence of a suitor who brought pizza and flowers for me at home, Wilson good-humoredly ate a slice of pizza and casually asked the visitor who brought said pizza if he, too, wanted a slice.

On normal days, Wilson's courtship style is like this: I usually stayed up till midnight since I needed to read my law books. It was during those intervals that Wilson would go back to his barracks at Camp Vicente Lim, Laguna from a whole day of activities with his boss. As soon as he's free, usually by midnight or late night, he would call and text informing me that he just got back to his quarters. After 30 minutes to an hour, he would text me, again, to ask if it's okay to visit me. Our conversations usually sounded like this:

Wilson on Phone: *Hi! I just got back here in the camp. The general had a long meeting at Shangri-La, that's why, blah, blah,blah... (end of conversation).*

A few minutes after, he would call again without telling me that he's already outside our gate.

All right, for you to get to relate better, let me give you an exact instance which recurrently happened:

Time: 1:45 a.m.

Wilson on Phone: Hi! I wonder if it's all right to visit you now.

Me: It's late. And sorry, I'm studying.

Wilson: Please allow me to see you even for 10 minutes, and I'll leave immediately, promise.

Me: Hmmm...10 minutes, are you sure? Okay!

Wilson: Thanks. Can you please open the gate for me since I'm already here outside? Hurry up, please, as mosquitos are starting to hound me.

So, he was actually already outside our door when he asked permission to visit me.

And it happened repeatedly.

My reaction? Grinning, stunned, impressed and slowly falling for him.

One time, with Wilson's usual visiting routine, my dad by coincidence woke up and went to see in the living room who my avid visitor was at around 3:00 am. It was the first time I officially introduced Wilson to my dad, since he used to visit me at midnights or super late nights. Thank goodness that my suitor Inspector Doromal was wearing a nice set of barong since he went straight to our house from a social function with Gen. Managuelod.

Yes, Wilson constantly visited me almost every midnight and followed me in shoots and other engagements whenever he's done with his work. It was then that I noticed that he had a special talent and charisma to get along well and easily with the people close to me, such as my cousins, friends, and the rest.

Never did this devoted suitor grumble about travelling to Manila from the camp and to the camp from Manila just to visit me and spend time with me for a maximum of only one hour. He didn't complain about having to join his boss for jogging every 5:00 am despite his lack of sleep. As a side note, Inspector Wilson said he was clever enough to take a nap (to get to recover from sleepless nights) either during their travel time to Manila from Camp Vicente Lim in Laguna or during the day on waiting interludes for his boss, whenever the latter had meetings.

Meanwhile, some superiors in the Camp were suspecting that Inspector Doromal was seeing some GROs at night. They noticed that he had the habit of leaving the camp late at night and returning just before sunrise. Hence, the junior officer was scolded by the then Chief Inspector Victorino Mina who, like a father, cautioned him to watch his actions. It's hilarious that our then soon-to-be wedding godfather had no idea who Wilson was visiting every night.

And though it's funny how Inspector Doromal was prejudged in different occasions, it's likewise admirable of him not to say any word to defend himself.

Likewise, worth it is to recall that while we were still at the getting-to-know stage, I often accused Wilson of lying. In all those instances, he wouldn't debate with me. He would just normally clarify the situation briefly and would stop talking afterwards. Lucky me as with that kind of attitude, we never had any single argument.

There was an occasion where Wilson said he would call me as soon as he gets back to his home in Quezon City. A day had passed and he didn't call me and his mobile phone was out of coverage. At that moment, I was proactive enough to assume that he went somewhere without informing me, or that he was cheating on me, that's why he turned his cellphone off.

Having exposed with all kinds of deceits and liars in my previous work as intelligence consultant for four years working on various confidential cases at Tax Fraud, Bureau of Internal Revenue, no matter how I thought about Wilson's enlightenments, I was skeptical. Despite that, the young Inspector Doromal endeavored to gently familiarize me to the fact he's the type who could sleep for 24 hours (perhaps, due to the nature of his stressful job where he lacked sleep) and that he honestly didn't turn his mobile off. It's just that his room in the house had very poor signal.

As expected of a typical woman, I was cynical about his words before, but, when we got married, I realized that indeed, Wilson could sleep for 24 hours straight. And exactly as he said, the signal in his room is really poor until today.

In many occasions in our life as single, I was guilty of silently accusing Wilson of lies, where in the end, he was proven to have stated the truth. I am emphasizing the doubts versus honesty aspect of our story because honesty has such a great weight in our, so far, seventeen years of marriage.

CHAPTER FOUR

The Marriage of Tsip and Kumander

November 11, 2000— Three hours before my wedding, the back portion of my wedding gown was accidentally burned by the hotel staff while pressing it. Hahah! Oh yeah, it created a huge, unpardonable hole at the back. Can you imagine how we were able to handle it? My mom thought it was a joke. Hilarious! It created a prodigious panic among the family members who were all set for the church.

Grace Under Pressure. Still fresh it is in my memory the scene when I was fleeing from the Fanny Serrano Salon (my hair and makeup sponsor) with hair curlers on to fit a new gown in every promising boutique at the Makati Cinema Square. I did it all by myself, and so everyone was looking for me. I ended up getting the only piece that fit me, but never matched the color of my veil. Opportunely, my veil was multi-layered and long enough to cover the life-size hole on my original gown. It worked! By no means had anyone of my guests ever noticed it!

The Rewarding Experience. I can't help but cherish our Filipiniana Police Officer's Christian nuptial with only a month of preparation and attended by nearly 450 guests. Special thanks to 7107 Islands Traveller's Club for the free hotel accommodations at The Philippine Plaza (now Sofitel), Rembrandt, Sulo, Legenda, Boracay Terraces and Silver Place.

It's been seventeen years now and I feel how our marriage has matured. Tsip and I never had any serious fight and we never had any unresolved issues. Thanks for the unchanging love—though with some touches of acts of disloyalty accompanied by fearless honesty in between, hahah — respect, transparency and understanding by my officer and gentleman.

I have all the reasons to be grateful that I've been enjoying every bit of my married life. My ex- boyfriend Wilson and I didn't have a long engagement; but definitely, we met at the right season in our life.

I was 27 turning 28 in two months at that time, Mass Communication graduate, an advertising executive of my small marketing and advertising company, tv host and pursuing law. Wilson was 28, Business Administration and BS Public Safety graduate, holds the rank of police inspector and pursuing his MBA. Let's say, we were both "single, free and searching" at that stage, hahah! Now, we are even closer to each other as we remain the best of friends with our two sons around: Ezekiel Wilson, 15, and Zecheriah Wilson, 11-years old.

Ideology on Marriage. Marriage is a permanent union both under the Philippine law and under the law of God. For me, it is a decision and a destiny. How you live happily within it is a bilateral effort between the husband and wife.

In our case, Tsip and I unconditionally support each other's endeavors, whims and caprices irrespective of our limitations. Interestingly, we never clash on financial issues, we never worry about tomorrow; moreover, we both enjoy sharing our blessings to everyone around us as a matter of passion. Without pretentions, we are both social entrepreneurs who can extend help with gladness at anyone without expecting any favor in return.

Note that I wasn't aware of these features prior to marrying Tsip. I'm not also saying that ours is the best style of relationship to emulate. All I know is that my marriage came to me as a blessing. Most important of all, our ultimate secret is acknowledging the Almighty in every aspect of our life. The real strength comes from our daily dose of prayer and meditation of God's Word.

Realizations. I went over my two-hour wedding video, and more than the entertainment part and comical bloopers, etcetera, I got to realize so many things which steered me to be even more grateful to

God for all his favor to me and my family. In that video, I saw friends and relatives who have gone a long way.

Some of the little kids and shower girls then are now professionals. My male secondary sponsors from PNPA Kapanalig Class of '97 who were police inspectors at that time are already police superintendents (colonel) today. Also, there are those among our guests who already left to live permanently abroad, such as my in-laws, relatives, one of the officiating ministers, and friend Aris who served as the bridal car driver and an instant "principal sponsor. Furthermore, there were special people who have departed for good and are now with the Lord —for instance, my grandfather, grandmothers, principal sponsor Congressman Ponce, a cousin and an aunt and an uncle.

Truly, we can never rewind a single second of our life, neither can we add even half a second to it...but, we can always treasure beautiful memoirs.

Expectations. May the Lord allow us to live a long, happy and significant life that we may, as a complete family, perform our passions and calling: "To learn, lead, teach, serve, influence and inspire".

The past seventeen years of our marriage has brought us diverse forms of life experiences and lessons which may aptly be called wisdom today. On the next chapters of this book, I will try, as much as I can, to share miscellaneous inspirational true-to-life tales, in no particular sequence of occurrence, which I hope to edify and encourage our readers.

Break time: Positivity Check

You were given a 500 ml bottle containing 250 ml water in it. What do you say? The glass is half full or half empty? Insufficient or just enough?

I would say: "It is enough to be shared"! –Kumander Misis

CHAPTER FIVE

Tips to Betrayed Spouses

We were blessed with two sons in the family: Ezekiel Wilson, whom we call "Zekie", who's now 16 and Zecheriah Wilson, whom we call "Strong," who's now 12 years old.

Back in 2003 when Zekie was a toddler, and Strong wasn't born yet, I would frequent the United States to explore business opportunities.

At first, I incorporated a public relations and marketing business in Las Vegas where through that, I had the chance to produce various events in the US, and to publish The Phil Am Press newspaper in Daly City, and in Los Angeles for the Southern CA Edition. But, upon seeing Zekie via Skype that he was turning pale despite having a dedicated nanny taking care of him; plus, noticing Tsip to had lost weight as well, I decided to rush back home forthwith. From then on, I decided to devote most of my time taking care of the family. Until today.

For that reason, I would always say that motherhood is my primary career. All other dealings are simply hobbies or sidelines or A.I.D.S., as in Acquired Income Due to Sideline, in order to sustain my motherhood career! Having said that, you could expect that I have such an excellent bond with my kids and husband.

Just now, I stumbled upon some childhood videos of my boys while I was reviewing my old page posts to take inspiration for two speaking engagements for this week—one as regards my "Progressive Education" advocacy, and the other, "The Journey of Motherhood." Timely it is to discuss something about womanhood as we are currently celebrating the International Women's Month.

Checking on my posts, I realized how time flies that Zekie will be celebrating, again, his birthday next month. Why does it seem like the speed of time is always set on turbo? This coming school year, he will be in senior high where technically, during our time, that's equivalent to college freshman already. A few more days, Zekie will turn 16 already. Imagine that!

Anyway, I can't help but look back at my pregnancy where people would always appreciate the bearing and style of a "hot pregnant teenager" (as they thought). Weeeeh! But, actually, I was already in super late 20s when I got married. That is, turning 28 years old in two months after our marriage!

To continue my pregnancy story, I wore high heels and mini skirt up to the very day I was to be sent to the delivery room. Next, I was admitted to the hospital on the night of April 11, 2001. Feeling bored during the first stages of my labor, the then Inspector Wilson Doromal and I had gone out of the hospital to go shopping at the nearby SM Mall –meaning, we escaped from the hospital; and definitely, I was wearing my heels! (Warning: Please don't try it at home. Only highly trained professionals can do that! Hahah!).

While strolling along the cosmetics section, a neighbor-friend saw me and said: "Oh, I didn't know you're pregnant! When is your due date?"

ME: Actually, today. And I'm currently on labor.

Neighbor: What a sassy girl you are! And, girl, you are in heels! (She kept on laughing out loud)

A few moments from our short escape from the hospital, my Momski Mercedita received a call at home. It was the hospital staff looking for me.

April 12, 2001, Maundy Thursday, my 8.7-pound Ezekiel Wilson was born! Everybody was excited as he was the first grandchild.

In three weeks, my figure got back to 26-inch-waistline. 23.5 inches prior to pregnancy. Though today, I'm sorry to say that I no longer measure my waistline!

Praise the Lord for your birth, life, health and for every amazing favor He gives you, Zekie Doromal! Needless it is to say how much we love you!

If there be three things which I appreciate the most about Zekie, those are his being responsible, respectful and compassionate. He is someone who has extreme sensitivity and high regard of other people's feelings. For instance, he doesn't utter anything (especially to me) without thinking first if the same is appropriate or not. He has his own charismatic way of expressing his most profound and most curious thoughts at the proper time and settings and through proper channels. There are times where he would ask me, "Mom, how can I say this to them without offending them?"

By nature, unlike the typical teens, he never ever abuses his privileges. He's been like that since childhood. I remember during his toddler years where I would ask Zekie what he wanted as gift... He would say, "nothing" or "none"... And one time, he requested, "Judge, Mom!" "What Judge?, I asked. Then I learned it's a chewing gum brand that he saw on tv. Afterwards, I asked how many pieces of Judge, wherein he answered quickly, "only one!"

How cool it is that Zekie appreciates our "YESes" on his infrequent requests and humbly accepts our "NOes". He never splurges on anything even if we give him our ATM or shopping money. He doesn't feel nor sound "entitled", which is, by the way, an impression about him shared and confirmed with me by a luminary. He's more of a doer than a talker.

How blessed we are to have a son like you, Zekie! May the Lord's unceasing guidance and protection be with you in everything that you think and do.

Although I'm generally pleased and grateful about what's going on with my life, I must admit that I, somehow, have this ambivalence towards seeing the kids grow up in a flash.

In a matter of years, the children become adults, and reality dictates they will have to walk their way to the future by themselves. Hahah, separation anxiety attacks the mom this early!

Anyway, I'm inspired to write this topic for special friends who are currently undergoing tight circumstances in their marriage and family life. A number of Facebook friends would message me regularly to ask for advice on love and marriage, thinking that mine is a perfect marriage and that I'm in authority to give sound advice.

First off, "thanks for the trust." Secondly, "mine is not a perfect marriage," and lastly, "... but, we have a perfect God in this family that makes this marriage survive life's situations where we learn together as a couple each day."

Having been married to a police officer, it's quite a challenge that I have to take extra efforts to balance my level of understanding, support and love to my better half versus my personal priorities and major decisions which we have to take as a couple—from where to establish our residence and how long, where to send the kids in school, whether to work, or be a full-time homemaker, and so forth. We are aware that a single decision may strengthen or be a threat to the family life; therefore, Tsip and I decided to set and work towards our priorities, bearing in mind their long term repercussions in the family.

Since the lifetime of an officer is a realizable daily journey on roads to temptations attacking family and personal values, working on a strong relationship is an enduring process.

One of the worst challenges to a faithful woman is when her Mr. Right becomes Mr. Left.

When it happens, think right, re-route as needed and go straight ahead to your destination!

But, actually, it doesn't really matter what your husband's profession is, whether he is a businessman, a politician or a street sweeper, temptations or the so-called "test of values" are everywhere. Why? Because we're on earth, we can't choose the situations and people we bump into each day. The test of one's character emanates along the way. Hence, the wife has a special role in guiding her husband and in bringing the husband back to his senses, just in case the latter derails from his values.

Girls, I feel like I have so much in my heart to share, but for now, let me simplify the points into two, which are:

1. **Trust your spouse.** Love cannot stand alone without trust. It's the foundation of a smooth and lasting relationship. Otherwise, your home will be jam-packed with paranoia, pointless fights, baseless terror, and tension. However, by trust, I don't mean being vulnerable to being cheated. Therefore, go ahead, wives, check on the whereabouts and activities of your husbands—in a nice way!

When Tsip was assigned as Deputy Regional Chief of Highway Patrol Group Region 3 (that covers Pampanga, Bulacan, Zambales, Bataan, Nueva Ecija, Tarlac, Aurora), he stayed in Camp Olivas Pampanga most of his weekdays and would come to Manila only on weekends. I couldn't stay with Tsip in the camp and sacrifice our children's education at that time as both of our kids were full academic scholars at a prestigious international school. In other words, I completely assumed the responsibility to be with our kids the whole time. Nevertheless, I would, of course, check on Wilson's whereabouts every now and then.

One late night, I called Tsip and asked what he was doing wherein he said that he was in a coffee shop and about to go back to his quarters. As we were talking and about to hang up the phone, I heard a human police siren (human horn) seemingly seated beside Tsip jokingly yelling: "wang...wang...wang..." Hence, I caught that they were still out.

So, husbands, remember that it's your wife's right to know your engagements as she's your other half. It's a basic act of love and respect that you are transparent to your wife. Moreover, it will help keep away worries. Take it as a proactive approach to help you resist or prevent bad choices, should there be any.

1. **Expect the best, but be ready for the worst.** To think that you'll separate or go on divorce one day isn't proper. Scientifically, biblically and medically speaking, positive thinking yields multifarious benefits. And so, it's all worthwhile to think positive and to practice the "law of attraction" with respect to your marriage.

Alright, you have a picture of a perfect relationship in your head. But what if your husband betrays your trust?

Compose yourself for a tough decision. And here, you will have to decide on a personal and case-to-case basis. Are you willing to keep the relationship or are you leaving your husband? Will you treat yourself as a victim or as a survivor?

Upon weighing the ins and outs of the circumstance, and assuming you decided to keep your relationship and be a "survivor" rather than a "victim" of betrayal, anticipate an arduous process that you have to go through. Then contemplate on the following:

a. **Counseling.** You may need counseling from a respected confidante, a trusted minister or a marriage counselor. For counseling sessions on how to go about the process, I would recommend that the spouses go together, so that both sides may be heard, for better understanding of the situation, and for mutual support.

Furthermore, as much as possible, don't go to your parents or parents-in-law to disparage your spouse, as more often than not, it creates a lasting vilifying impression against the erring party and in the end, impairing the family relationship.

b. **Pray without ceasing.** Don't expect that experiencing betrayal will be that easy to forget. Certainly, the same may haunt you all throughout your life. For that reason, the best weapon is prayer. And that is: Pray when alone. Pray with your husband. Pray with your family. What's good about praying is that it has no inhibitions— cry, shout, whisper, sing... it's up to you. And it works!

c. **Forgive. Totally!** I know this is much easier said than done; nevertheless, without total forgiveness, there will be no healing. Without forgiveness, you cannot move on with your life, even after hundreds of years.

Forgiveness is a crucial stage of the show where you and your husband will have to be strong partners rather than enemies. Although, betrayal is never right, not something you deserve, and is never fair in all respects, the situation is not only about you. In reality, your husband is also struggling within himself due to guilt and desire to win your trust back. As regards this, I would like to share that you try to drown your spouse with kindness no matter what happens.

Reputable psychologists, behavioral scientists, and educators agree, and I certainly agree with them, that humans are naturally capable of learning from their mistakes and experiences; furthermore, they are capable of changing for the better. I hope you would consider that.

Finally, once you totally forgive, go back to No. 1 (Trust your spouse) and No. 2 (Expect the best and be ready for the worst).

How far have you been traveling in this life? How long will it take you to finish your journey? How important is your marriage to you? How much do you value your family?

Life is a short and temporary cycle of (1) trust and distrust (2) expectations (3) fulfillment or disappointment and (4) forgiveness and unforgiveness. And regardless of our individual differences and personal choices, there is only one ultimate rule that binds the entire humanity: love.

CHAPTER SIX

Back to Basics

I was invited to speak before a congregation of a small community Christian church in Manila last Sunday. And in my attempt to prepare the message, I was waiting for a perfect internet connection last weekend whereby, for whatever reason, all my internet providers at home failed to give me a stable internet access. I'm not sure, though, if it's only in the Philippines that we experience it.

Therefore, I ended up manually outlining my message using a recycled notebook, pen and my Bible—not the electronic one. It was a realization that despite full exposure to modernization, we couldn't rely on technology all the time; hence, the best thing is to get back to basics.

Yes, "Back to Basics" had been our topic which I'm simplifying into this writing today.

My hope is that we all learn from the book of Ecclesiastes which was authored by no less than King Solomon, who also wrote the books Proverbs and Song of Songs.

King Solomon, son of King David, as we know, was blessed with unsurpassed wisdom, with bonuses of power and riches, allowing him to rule over Israel for 40 years. He enjoyed life at its fullest—drinking wine, rejoicing, and having, literally, a thousand wives and mistresses. Many scholars believe that King Solomon died in his 60s, calculating that he began his kingship at about 20 years old or less, and ruled Israel for forty years.

With his stature and wisdom, what else could a King Solomon ask for? In Ecclesiastes 1, we can see that after all his achievements and glory, King Solomon was at a point of consciousness that everything is life is meaningless. Probably, what he was experiencing is comparable to some signs of midlife crisis that people in their late 40s experience today. In verse 3, he said: "What does man gain from all his labor at which he toils under the sun?" And in Chapter 12, the last chapter of Ecclesiastes, the author clearly emphasized the need for us to remember our Creator in the days of our youth. He ended up saying that ultimately, the whole duty of man is to "fear God and to keep His commandments", because every work, good or bad, exposed or done in secret will be judged in time.

Back to basics!

Academically, I finished four courses already, plus one honorary degree, and at present, concurrently taking up another masters and a diploma program. Not to mention that I'm a wife and a mom, too. Busy huh? Having said these, the story of King Solomon allowed me to contemplate on my most important title: "Servant of my Father God". That is the basic me, which I need to fully assess continually, and while I am still physically strong.

In reality, no matter what we do, what we achieve, and wherever we go, at the end of the day, we will get back to basics. I agree with King Solomon when he opined that he had achieved much, and at the prime of his life, what he sowed would be reaped by others. The thing is that life is a cycle and all our accomplishments will be forgotten in time.

Are you not stunned by the luxurious outfits celebrities wear on awards night? Or the fashion outfits worn by international models? No matter how sophisticated and expensive the evening wears celebrities put on, at the end of the day, these superstars will go to bed with the simplest and most comfortable outfits, with no makeup on and with only the basic sleeping wears as they retire at night.

Getting back to basics...

Remember what we learned during our pre-school and kindergarten years, where we were trained to distinguish the difference of everything in terms of color, size and number? "Encircle the biggest." "Which is the tallest?" Things like that. So that, later in life, we will get to be scrupulous in observing our day-to-day experiences and get used to knowing or perceiving which is right or wrong. In the same way, we get to become good writers by applying the basic knowledge of the alphabet and spelling which we learned in elementary years.

King Solomon knew the basic law in his heart since day one. Before inheriting the throne, his father King David reminded him to always follow God's decrees and commands (1 Kings 2:3-4). However, along the way, Solomon broke specific commandments God gave to the future kings of Israel such as: "Neither shall he multiply wives for himself, lest his heart turn away" Deuteronomy 17:17, among others.

None of us is above the law! For instance, one may temporarily fight aging—which is a law of nature—through botox, stem cell therapy, cosmetic surgery, and so forth. Those processes may only take effect for a moment; but, in the long run, the law of nature will prevail. Meaning, all signs of physical deterioration will be visible, whether we like it or not.

Just like Solomon, we are kings of our lives. And due to numerous priorities we are busy at, we tend to forget that we are governed by different laws which we cannot get away from—the law of nature, the law of man, and the law of God. With our fast-paced and high-tech lifestyle today, may we learn to set aside our vanity and decide to get back to basics.

Are you Forgetting Something?

"Car keys, gun, cellphone, 2-way radio, mobile charger"—these are the things my hubby often forgets to bring with him; thus, causing minutes of delay whenever he leaves for work. From then on, like a chant, I would habitually say: "keys-gun-cellphone-radio-charger" just before Tsip leaves. That is to make sure he's ready, with all basic gadgets complete!

But, not until we heard the message in the church where we were reminded to pray at all times. Praying is a basic need, just like food, water and clothing. By not praying, we impliedly say that we don't need God in our life...that every accomplishment is through our own work, and that every blessing we receive is something we deserve because we are good enough!

Though we have regular family devotion at night (Daily Hope by Rick Warren, plus family prayer), we didn't have a family morning prayer. This is something we had started upon hearing that message. Why? Because we acknowledge that we need the Lord in our life and in our family... That without Him, we are nothing! Having that in mind, from to then on, my chant had changed to this: "Prayer-keys-gun-cellphone-radio-charger."

Are there things you often forget in your life? Is prayer one of those? Start and end your day with a simple prayer from the heart and witness God's mighty work in your life. Let's all go back to basics.

If you have time, read the whole book of Ecclesiastes; it's only 12 chapters, anyway.

And before we end up, let me leave you these words of wisdom from King Solomon:

Ecclesiastes 2:4-11

4 I undertook great projects: I built houses for myself and planted
vineyards. 5 I made gardens and parks and planted all kinds of fruit
trees in them. 6 I made reservoirs to water groves of flourishing trees. 7
I bought male and female slaves and had other slaves who were born in
my house. I also owned more herds and flocks than anyone in Jerusalem
before me. 8 I amassed silver and gold for myself, and the treasure of
kings and provinces. I acquired male and female singers, and a harem
as well—the delights of a man's heart. 9 I became greater by far than
anyone in Jerusalem before me. In all this my wisdom stayed with me.
10 I denied myself nothing my eyes desired; I refused my heart no
pleasure.My heart took delight in all my labor,and this was the reward
for all my toil. 11 Yet when I surveyed all that my hands had done
and what I had toiled to achieve, everything was meaningless, a chasing
after the wind; nothing was gained under the sun.

And in Ecclesiastes 12:13-14: 13 Now all has been heard; here is the conclusion of the matter: Fear God and keep his commandments, for this is the duty of all mankind. 14 For God will bring every deed into judgment, including every hidden thing, whether it is good or evil.

Break time: Positivity Check

Learning is an attitude. It takes ears longing to hear, eyes open for discoveries, spirit willing to aspire and pride eager to be set right. – Kumander Misis

CHAPTER SEVEN

Pass the Message

Nearly thirty years ago, we used to play a game called "Pass the Message" where the leader would whisper a message, such as "supercalifragilisticexpialidocious" to two contending team leaders who would each pass the message to the next person in his team, until the message reaches the last member of the team who would shout out the message. Other than the speed, the message to be passed and shouted out has to be correct and precise; otherwise it's useless.

Exactly a year after I wrote my blogs entitled "Through the Strong Winds Part 1" and "Through the Strong Winds Part 2 (Learning from an Eagle in Pain)", I realized that the very words I wrote were meant for me the same month and day a year after. The blogs disclosed the incredible strengths of an eagle, as well as the ironic unimaginable weakness and pain it suffers during the molting process where the supposed robust eagle becomes helpless, necessitating support from stronger eagles. For you to get to relate better, after this chapter, I will be sharing those two blogs with you on the next two succeeding chapters.

Recently, the eagle in me got into its molting stage, that one night, I was so anxious that I couldn't even open my Bible, nor utter a prayer. It was at this fretful time that my husband sat beside me, opened the "Our Daily Bread", read for me God's message, shared his insights, and led me into a prayer. Incidentally, the text was my life verse Isaiah 40:30-31 saying: "Even youths grow tired and weary, and young men stumble and fall; but those who hope in the Lord will renew their strength. They will soar on wings like eagles; they will run and not grow weary, they will walk and not be faint." Then I remembered the previous blogs I mentioned above and read them once again. Here, I had a different appreciation of my writing. I felt like they were not authored by me and that the Lord was talking to me directly.

God's message is always clear. Though it comes in many forms — direct, indirect, Bible, life's circumstances, through nature, through media, and even in dreams, and so forth—it's always timely, correct and precise. The language of God in our lives is personal and specific to every individual. No one could interpret and understand your clear-cut personal communication with God except you.

My husband and I regularly attend Sunday Worship with our children. During the message part, I noticed that my kids who were twelve and eight years old at that time would grab their Iphone units and would concentrate on somewhat texting or gaming gesture. I called on my kids' attention one time, and I was surprised that contrary to what I thought, they were not texting or playing. They were actually writing their own notes while listening to the Pastor's message. It's a moment of discovery that my kids, at their own level, could write well and fast, hahah. And more importantly, I discovered that they understood what's being preached. The screenshot of Strong's notes dated March 23, 2014 are still saved on my phone. For the record and without edits, I would like to share the same with you by transcribing it below. I would love to attach the actual photos of the notes, but I'm not sure if the format would be acceptable on this e-book.

8-year old Strong wrote in his notes:

Bread that Gives Life

"Jesus made the bread that gives life. He made it so we will keep his trust and hope. Jesus is our savior which he always saves us for us. He loves us, he is the lover of our soul of course not the bad soul, and he is mighty. Jesus is the Son of God. Did you notice that? Being kind to others is what God and Jesus wants, for ex: You see a poor child. Don't ignore him/her. Because if you ignore that's a bad thing. The bread of life is made in Middle English in olden times. If you're a Christian and not in the church all day, you're not worshipping God. Remember that because it's

very important. Follow God's rules, learn from the church or Youtube. It's good when you're a Christian. And pray everytime when you're going to sleep, when you're going to eat. We all do that. Read the Bible also."

By Strong

He added after he signed his name, *"About bread that gives life trying to have a pure good heart. Being happy not always sad, not having a bad devilish heart"*

Certainly, the innocence and purity of Zecheriah's writing had touched my soul beyond grammatical construction, beyond punctuations, and so much beyond vocabulary.

One significant lesson I learned in this life is that sometimes it takes silence to get to hear clearly what God says. And in all cases, an open heart!

John 10:14 says, *"I am the good shepherd; I know my sheep and my sheep know me", and verses 2 and 16 mention that the sheep recognize the voice of their shepherd. In the same way, when we listen to the Lord our Shepherd and follow His voice, we will never go wrong."*

Like a child, may we listen to the words of our Father, all the days of our lives.

Hebrews 4:12 *For the Word of God is alive and active, sharper than any double-edged sword, it penetrates even to dividing soul and spirit, joints and marrow; it judges the thoughts and attitudes of the heart.*

2 Timothy 3:16-17 *All Scripture is God-breathed and is useful for teaching, rebuking, correcting and training in righteousness, so that the servant of God may be thoroughly equipped for every good work.*

Break time: Positivity Check

Wisdom and learning are both ageless. Whereas wisdom has no bounds, learning should be an unsatisfied appetite and a lifelong craving.—Kumander Misis

CHAPTER EIGHT

Through the Strong Winds

Did it ever occur in your life that you were at your "happily ever after" moment when a sudden nightmare came to attack the scene? And worse, what you thought was a nightmare turned out to be real?

There are various nauseating truths in life which make us anxious; and every human being has his own share of sweet, rancid, bitter realities given in different dosages, at altered stages and levels... by Destiny.

Tsip had borne many winds in his life from childhood till the time he entered the police academy. It was the then Cadet Wilson Doromal's first month in the Philippine National Police Academy (PNPA) when his dad passed away. And I can just imagine the double torment he had to go through at that time. According to stories, Wilson's waistline had shrunk to 23 inches that even his Aunts didn't recognize him during the wake.

As a matter of reflection, I just wanted to say that we only bury the physical body; but we don't bury our love and respect for the departed ones. In Christian faith, we believe in eternal life through Christ Jesus alone. This is the good news that brings us peace and hope that, someday, we shall have a grand reunion with our loved ones who went ahead of us to meet our Creator.

Despite Tsip's apparent success in his, so far, twenty-three years in service as police officer, he would always look back at the strong winds in his life which never swayed his faith and strength.

In a Facebook post, Tsip wrote this message on Father's Day in remembrance of his source of inspiration, his dad:

"Dear Tatay,

I found this photo while arranging some bits and pieces in my office; and my memory took me to the time when you were serving at the

Philippine Constabulary/ Integrated National Police (PC-INP). I remember you in uniform, as well as in plain white shirt and trunks at home. I remember you watering the plants, feeding the hogs and giving a sweet treat to your horses. I also remember how our family of six children would tag along with you everywhere you were assigned—in Camp Castaneda, Camp Crame, Pampanga, Iloilo etcetera.

That owner type jeep in the photo had taken us to many places. I remember my childhood where I used to sleep at the back of that jeep during the countless times that I waited for you to finish your work. You knew that I just always wanted to be with you and follow you everywhere you went... and I was happy.

Thanks for training me, Tatay, to be diligent and hardworking; that to my college years, you had me work with you as part-time security officer of our security agency, until such time that I obtained my degree Bachelor of Business Administration.

In 1995,during my training just after a month from my admission as cadet to the Philippine National Police Academy (PNPA), you passed away, leaving us with the greatest amount of wealth that we enjoy today, and that we would surely pass on to your decendants— our values!

Yes, today the world celebrates Father's Day; but, in my heart I give you tribute and thanks every single day.

Accept my salute, Col. Nelson C. Doromal, Sir!

Happy Father's Day to all! Special mention to my kindhearted father-in-law!"

It's already more than twenty years now from this specific heavy wind (dad's death) in the then young cadet's life. Just like anyone else, Tsip went through many winds and storms of life after that. But, through God's guidance, he stood still.

Isaiah 40:30-31 King James Version (KJV) say:

"*Even the youths shall faint and be weary, and the young men shall utterly fall: But they that wait upon the Lord shall renew their strength;*

they shall mount up with wings as eagles; they shall run, and not be weary; and they shall walk, and not faint."

Beautiful! The above verses are two of my all-time Biblical favorites. And if I may share, in times of distress, I always see myself as an eagle, reminding me of the "Eagle Christian" teaching.

Throughout the Bible, God compares Himself and His children to an eagle, where He safeguards, feeds and teaches His children in the same manner as an eagle defends, feeds and teaches the eaglets.

The word "eagle" is mentioned about 32 times in the Bible. God uses such metaphors and analogies to make us better understand spiritual things.

Are you an Eagle Christian?

It has been observed that unlike other birds, the eagle is never shaken by the storm. In fact, it has a special ability to sense the impending storm before it comes... and so, the eagle is ready for it.

While ordinary birds run and hide from the storm, the eagle bravely flies right into the storm and utilizes its currents to rise and fly higher. In other words, eagles use the storm to reach higher places. The moment an eagle finds the direction of the wind, it stops flapping its wings (time to rest!) and uses the force of the raging storm to mount into the clouds and glide.

An eagle Christian recognizes his authority through the Word of God, and is certain of his position—seated with Christ Jesus at the right hand of the Father—as a child of God. Hence, when trials come, a Christian faces them boldly in prayer. His life is composed.

Eagle versus Chicken

What would you rather be? An eagle or a chicken?

Complacent Christians are like chickens who accept trials defenselessly, without the power to overcome them. Like chickens, their wings are infantile and they cannot fly. They may have heard of and recognize the Word of God theoretically in their minds, but they do not have an intimate relationship with God; therefore, incapable to apply the Biblical principles.

Investing our time in the Word of God and in prayer will enable us to know how to effectively fight and win spiritual and real life battles.

CHAPTER NINE

Learning from an Eagle in Pain

Did you know that the eagle goes through a painful, depressing phase called the molting process? At this point, calcium deposits accumulate on the eagle's nails and beak with the eagle's feathers falling out. It is during this period that the originally robust eagle begins to walk like a turkey that it cannot hold its head up.

Imagine a majestic eagle who, at this time, has no strength to fly, has no vision (blind), cannot hunt for food, and regresses into the valley. Miserable, isn't it?

Amazingly, however, it is also in this period that the other eagles which have already gone successfully through the molting process will help the weak eagle to regain its strength. The strong eagles will fly above the valley to drop fresh food for the recuperating fellow eagle.

Not all eagles are successful. Those who do not get help from other eagles will eventually die in the valley. But as to those who recover their strength, they will climb the mountain in which they were raised, where they will then fly on the rock, and beat the calcium deposits off their beaks and talons. Although, this is a very painful experience that eagles have to go through, after this agony, the eagle will soar again with greater strength, and will be even more majestic than ever before!

During our earlier years of marriage, Tsip and I had tried to explore business opportunities and investments in order to achieve our simple dreams of owning a more decent home, and providing the finest for ourselves and for our future children. With our little amount of savings, we distributed our funds and invested the same with various companies which promised us higher-than-usual yield. Since the dividends we were receiving at that time were much higher than the interest if we would take a loan, we decided to obtain a loan from the military bank and invested the proceeds to these companies promising us greater yield.

The business seemed well and normal at the onset; hence, we got our very first potential home in New Manila on a pre-selling scheme and had paid the equity and the monthly installments through our earnings from our investments. It was also through our earnings from these investments that we were able to get a new car, and other things beyond what we needed.

One weekend, while I was with Tsip on a training in Zambales, we heard a bad news from all other police officers who also had investments on those companies. The bad news was that the companies we invested our money on had simultaneously ceased their operations and the owners escaped. The news made a clamor all over the country, but the investors were helpless. In other words, we (and so are many police and military officers) got scammed. We had no option but to start from zero and accept that we were in serious debt.

It wasn't an easy situation, but, the strength, wisdom and provision of the Lord sustained us. So here we are today.

As eagle Christians, we are not exempt from going through the valley of troubles. Our strength is best appreciated when we go through trials and get to overcome them.

We should not fear.

Learn from King David when he said: *"Even though I walk through the darkest valley, I will fear no evil, for you are with me; your rod and your staff, they comfort me." (Psalms 23:4)*

We have to strengthen one another.

1 Thessalonians 5:11 says :*"Therefore encourage one another and build each other up, just as in fact you are doing."*

Ultimately, all of us draw our strength from our God through the Lord Jesus our "Rock".

Psalm 18:2 *The LORD is my rock, my fortress and my deliverer; my God is my rock, in whom I take refuge. He is my shield and the horn of my salvation, my stronghold.*

...And don't ever forget that you are an EAGLE!

Related Verses:

1 Corinthians 10:4 *And did all drink the same spiritual drink: for they drank of that spiritual Rock that followed them: and that Rock was Christ.*

Exodus 33:21 *Then the LORD said, "There is a place near me where you may stand on a rock.*

Exodus 19:4 *You have seen what I did to the Egyptians, and how I bore you on eagles' wings and brought you to Myself.*

Psalms 91:4 *He will cover you with his pinions, and under His wings you will find refuge; His faithfulness is a shield and buckler.*

CHAPTER TEN

How to Teach the Bible to Growing Kids

One common denominator between Zekie and Strong is that as toddlers, they both enjoyed reading the Bible and watching Bible stories online. As they have both developed this hobby, I'm blessed enough for not having to exert extra effort in convincing them to read what they used to call the "Super Book".

Strategy, of course, is another issue. How to make kids understand the Bible is an imaginative and creative task. Here are some ideas on how to teach the Bible to the little ones:

1. ***When to begin.*** Teaching the Bible to kids is not a difficult job to parents who start early. As we say: "Early bird catches the worm." Begin exposing your child to the Bible as early as possible. As soon as the child is exposed to Bible principles through relevant means, like Biblical songs or kids' praise, exposure grows into interest and interest forms a habit.

2. ***Where to begin.*** In teaching the Bible, start with the basic and most important character—God, the Supreme Being. It is really important to start right because this becomes the foundation of your child's faith. This may be effectively taught by starting with "creation" in the book of Genesis, where the power of God was shown when He created the world and everything in it. The next step is to introduce Jesus, which may be begun with a lesson on the promise of Savior to Mary through Angel Gabriel; to be followed by the story of the birth of Christ. For kids of all levels, the many miracles of Jesus Christ, which can be easily pictured or imagined, are ideal sequence of lessons.

3. ***Use visual aids to illustrate.*** Visual aids have three main purposes—to catch the kid's attention, for better comprehension and retention. If the kid is two to seven years old, use colored pictures to help him understand the story better. Online resources may also be

used. For kids older than seven years old, any form of visual aids, such as puppets, may be used.

4. ***Involve the kid.*** After telling a story, you may engage your child to helpful activities like games, creative arts, and drawing, in relation to the story he learned, for enhanced recall. If you have more than one kid, interactive activities may be done indoors and outdoors.

5. ***Memory verse.*** Since kids have good memory, take this opportunity to make them keep the Word of God in their hearts, while developing their memory skills, by having them memorize Biblical verses. Start with short verses, like Genesis 1:1,"In the beginning God created heaven and earth." As the child improves, you may have him try longer verses.

6. ***Helpful videos.*** One passive yet effective way to teach the Bible to your kids is to leave them alone in the room while watching Bible animation. To complete the feel, treat them with snacks, like what they would have in a movie house.

7. ***Bible story telling at bedtime.*** Instead of counting sheep before he sleeps, share a Bible story with your kid at bedtime. It doesn't have to be long, and it doesn't matter if you repeat similar stories many times. The logic here is to make God's Word a vital part of your kid's daily life.

8. ***Sunday School/Vacation Bible School.*** Since I'm a Sunday School baby, too, I can attest on how this experience has influenced me. Those I learned thirty years ago are still fresh in my memory.

While not all churches offer Sunday School sessions, when given an option to send your kid to Sunday School, or Friday School (such as in UAE) or Vacation Bible School classes, don't hesitate to have him join the class, even if you feel your child won't understand the lesson.

Trust that God will have your kid understand the Bible in due time. Isaiah 55:11 says, "*so is my word that goes out from my mouth: It will not return to me empty, but will accomplish what I desire and achieve the purpose for which I sent it.*"

Raising our kids in the knowledge of God is a wonderful decision. Let's take it from the great psalmist King David who said: *"Your word is a lamp to my feet and a light for my path."* (Psalm 119:105).

May the Word of God enlighten both our path as well as that of our kids, today and every day.

CHAPTER ELEVEN

Secrets to a Peaceful Family Home

For four years now, Tsip's assignment has been favorable to us in terms of saving his travel time from home to the office and vice versa. He is currently holding the post of Deputy Chief of Police for Administration of the City of Paranaque where we reside. The Police Station where Tsip goes to work every day is literally a stone's throw away from us. That is approximately 5-minute travel time. Therefore, Tsip can easily respond to emergencies 24/7.

The life of a police officer is such a busy, action-packed strenuous life and full of surprises. An officer may be assigned, as public service so requires, to anywhere in the Philippines.

Outside of our home, I expect that hubby's daily routine is filled with various cases, deployment, arrests, patrolling, meetings, conferences, personnel formation, administrative duties and concurrent operational compliances, and so forth. How did I know? Well, I am used to it since we've been together for 17 years now.

The challenge for a police officer's wife each day is to create a home atmosphere that is conducive to rest and encouragement for everyone in the family. Hubby had enough stress for the day working hard for the country and for the family; hence, he deserves peace.

Now, let me throw this question, how excited are you to coming home from work or school each day? Is your home the best place you can share your biggest smile, laugh at the top of your voice, and be tranquil whether awake or asleep?

How do we attain and maintain a peaceful home? Here are some tips:

1. ***Constant and proper communication.*** As in any other kind of relationship, regular communication is the key to

understanding your spouse, children or any other member of your family. Lack of communication draws you apart from one another, bringing about miscommunication, misunderstanding and declining relationship.

Yes, you might be the silent type. But that's not an excuse. A simple compliment like "You look wonderful" or a word of concern like "How's your day?" or "Have you eaten yet?" are powerful single-liners.

Communication may not, at all times, be expressed only in words. Text messages, sticky notes, a smile, a cup of coffee, hugs and kisses are gestures that communicate better relationships.

As to the other party, it's important that he/she takes time to LISTEN and is sensitive to what's being communicated to him/her.

1. ***Make time for your loved ones.*** Busy? Who wouldn't be busy in this millennium? Even our pets at home may be busy doing their own stuff.

Set aside a quality moment with your family. It doesn't matter how short or long each day, as long as your time and thoughts are exclusively devoted for your spouse or kids on that particular moment. It may be a 15-minute meal time without interruptions, or a two-hour movie time.

I noticed how gadgets intercept with our quality time and communication at home. For instance, dining out with the family is supposed to be dedicated for quality bonding and conversation among us. Being mindful of that, I would always caution my kids about their undesirable habit of using gadgets at the wrong time. If possible, get rid of your tabs and cellular phones when spending a family moment.

1. ***Renew your love every single day.*** It's sad to realize that a lot of people around the world feel like their own home is a battlefield where enemies are ready to strike from any corner. As a result, they end up seeking for comfort from the outside

world or other people where most likely, they engage themselves to vices.

Let's be realistic about it. Not all days are high. There are moments in our life where we feel low and depressed and struggling for whatever reason. The used-to-be enchanting before may not exhibit any charm at all in some aspects. And it's tough to renew our love to someone who's not loveable.

Another secret to achieving peace in your home is to fall in love with your spouse every single day. Don't let yourself be enticed by things which will ruin your relationship. Never get tired of rekindling the sweetness you had when you were at the peak of your happy relationship. Be aware though that this aspect is a mutual effort and responsibility between the couple.

4. ***Consider your family in making life's choices.*** Opportunities come and, sometimes, being overwhelmed with them makes us decide in a flash without thinking of consequences. Think wisely when making decisions and consult your spouse to be certain he's open about them and is willing to support you along the way.

5. ***Set rules but be reasonable.*** As parents, it's all right to set rules to our kids— no video games on school days, reward for a perfect grade, no smoking, etc. Be careful, though, in setting up rules, and be sure that your rules are workable. Give everyone a certain level of freedom to express themselves or their opinions. If your kids (especially the teens) look at you as a modern day Hitler whose wishes couldn't be challenged, chances are, your kids might rebel against you.

Many disorders at home are caused by rebellious acts and insubordination. Hence, let's be watchful on these tendencies.

6. ***Don't spread unhealthy rumors about your family.*** Every home has its own imperfection. Siblings clash and spouses disagree occasionally. Don't gossip about your own family because this will cause unlimited trouble for everyone.

7. ***Don't gossip about somebody else's life.*** It is a basic rule that we shouldn't meddle into the lives of other people. If you're not a party to issues outside of your home, and if you're not being requested to give sound advice, it would be best that you keep your mouth from talking. Just mind your own life issues to avoid sudden chaos from the people around. As in Kumander Misis' language: "Don't talk whenyour mouth is fool."

8. ***Settle issues as soon as possible.*** Should there be any disagreement in your family, resolve the problem as soon as possible. How soon? Within the day! This might sound irrational especially when the matter is a big issue. Call me extreme, but, I think there's nothing too big when we're talking about preserving peace in our own home. We're protecting our family relationship here.

Stop waiting for the right timing in the future because, most likely, pride will take its course the longer we wait. No reconciliation will be had. It's good to be guided by Biblical principles such as, "Be angry and do not sin; do not let the sun go down on your anger." (Eph. 4:26)

9. ***Desire peace.*** As love is a decision, peace is a decision, as well. "Think about" "say" and "do" things which will bring about peace into your home. Remember, what we sow is what we reap.

10. ***Pray with your family.*** This is the ultimate secret that I would like to impart. Pray with your family and ask God to take control of every situation in your life.

Praying together may not mean the family being physically together in one room. Many homes have family members in other places, for work or other reasons.

By praying together, it may mean setting a certain time of the day wherein everyone will pause for a moment to pray for the family, anywhere he may be. It may also mean praying at no specific time, where everyone shall pray for a common intention about the family.

"Trust in the LORD with all your heart and lean not on your own understanding; in all your ways acknowledge him, and he will make your paths straight." (Proverbs 3:5-6)

Breaktime: Positivity Check

"While words may be sharp as a sword; silence may be an artful killer."—Kumander Misis

CHAPTER TWELVE

How to Discipline a Child with Minimal or NO Spanking

Being blessed with two boys, I find it challenging for me as a mom to raise my two kids in a single standardized manner since they have two distinct personalities.

Disciplining the child is a skill that parents learn over the years of living with their kids. I believe, no one is ready enough to become a parent until he or she gets there.

In my approach of discipline, Proverbs 22:6 guides me along the way, where it says: "Train up a child in the way he should go: and when he is old, he will not depart from it." And as to how I apply the principle, please check these out:

1. ***Start early.*** Mold your child's ideal behavior as early in his life as possible. Developmental psychologists say that even the newborn has his own way of communicating his feelings and responding to mommy's voice and other sounds—cooing, gurgling, smiling, and crying. So, it is important that you communicate with your kid in a manner that he will understand.

For instance, a warm hug or kiss to a baby will mean love. Or to a first grader, how do you communicate good grooming? Do this by combing his hair, fixing his clothes, and putting on cologne before he goes to school, and say these simple words: "You look great. This is the way you should be every day."

Now that Ezekiel is already a teen, I appreciate it a lot how he was trained up to be respectful and responsible. Yesterday, for example, he went out with friends in Greenbelt. Before he even asked permission for a day out, he finished all his lessons and took his finals in all subjects first. He got pretty decent high grades, anyway. Then, before he left, he finished his Taekwondo training, fed his dog, cleaned his room, put the clothes in the washing machine and cleaned up the dry leaves in the backyard. When he was away, he texted me several times as to his whereabouts, the time he would come home and the plate number of the Grab he was riding on. I gave him more than enough amount of pocket money, but he came back home without spending it.

Again, starting early forms a habit.

1. ***Set an example.*** The general principle in disciplining the child is to "do what you preach." If you want something for your child to adopt, set an example. You may not effectively teach your child the bad effects of smoking if you frequently smoke in front of him.

1. ***Form a habit.*** *A* habit starts by introducing the right thing and doing the same thing constantly. For instance, if you want your child to eat vegetables, then, introduce to him vegetables by serving vegetables (such as carrots, cabbage, broccoli, etc.) regularly in his meals. In our family, it has been a habit to say "I love you" at one another many times in a day. Even if they're boys, my sons don't hesitate to be expressive in words and in actions. For instance, Strong would normally always ask: "Is there anything I can help you with, Mom?" Or Zekie would usually say: "Just go upstairs and take a rest, Mom. I'll take charge of everything."

1. ***Involve the child.*** A Chinese proverb says: "Tell me I will forget. Show me I will remember. Involve me and I will understand." The effects are poles apart in "simply saying swimming is fun", "having your child watch kids swimming", and "having your child dip himself in the pool to swim".

Educators and psychologists agree with similar principle that learning is attained most when the person is involved. In this manner, the person is able to tell others about his experience, and that experience will stick in his mind.

1. ***Make good things fun.*** Forcing your child to do something good may imply future negative repercussions, such as rebellion, insubordination, inability to decide for/by himself or hatred.

Better than pressing on him, think of fun ways of making him do something out of his own choice. For instance, in my case, I want my kids to be thoughtful. How do I train them to be thoughtful? When my sons were younger, for instance, I prepared a table complete with art materials—colorful pens, nice paper, scissors etc.—and asked the boys if they wanted to join me in creating Christmas cards for dad and granny. Yes, they joined me and were both excited to give their personalized Christmas cards to everyone.

1. ***Reward for good things done.*** The reward system, also known as positive reinforcement, is an excellent counterpart of corporal punishment or spanking. When your child does something good (even just simple ones, not necessarily outstanding acts), let him enjoy rewards. If he studied well, then let him play his favorite computer games on weekend.

1. ***Transform negative instructions into positive.*** Child psychologists believe that negative words and phrases like "no," "don't," "you can't," "I won't," "stop," and "not until" have unhelpful effects to the child.

> When a parent says "no," the child perceives the parent as a hindrance to what he wants to do. Parents are advised not to use these words, as much as possible, and just think of creative ways to speak their instructions. For instance, your child asks for chocolate candies right ahead of lunch. Instead of saying, "No chocolates until you've finished your lunch," you could say, "Sure, you can have chocolates after we've eaten lunch."

Whichever way we choose to discipline our children, it is important that we make them feel that we do it out of love.

CHAPTER THIRTEEN

How to Strengthen Parent-Teen Relationship

At the stage of puberty of your child, family support is highly demanded to assure that the parent-teen bond is not severed by the adjustments which occur in physical, emotional, intellectual, and social aspects of the child.

Every now and then, teenagers would ask for my advice though Facebook and Messenger as regards the common scenario of parents and teens clashing about various issues at home. Zekie would also sometimes ask me if it's okay to entertain at home for a sleepover his friends who have run away from home due to issues with their moms or dads.

I have observed from these cases that the issues are brought about mainly by the unreadiness of both parties—parents and children—to gracefully face the inevitable teenage stage. Conflict lies partly on age gap, lack of bonding or quality time spent together by the parents and teen, and severed by the fact that the adolescent often aggressively explores many new things about life, which in the eyes of the parents are foul or inappropriate. If parents would endeavor to reach out to strengthen their relationship with their teens, disagreements might be minimized. Check out these tips:

1. ***Be your teen's best friend.*** Parents should know when to eradicate their parental vest to give way to friendship with their children. Just like a real best friend, spend time with your teen as much as you can—laugh, eat, or even cry with him/her, go to the gym with him or go out on a salon or grooming party with your teen.. Take time to talk casually when you're together and as he comes home from school, ask how his day went. Be aware as well that the most common struggle among the parents and teens nowadays is communication. We

should have noticed how gadgets (phones, tabs, social media, games, and so on) interfere with our precious family moments. Consider a regular gadget-free dinner, karaoke time or quiet time with your family. It takes time, practice, effort and consistency in order to achieve this first tip.

2. ***Give your teen some freedom to act without your shadow.*** How do we reconcile this tip with number 1 above? It's important to know our limitations in interfering with the life and whereabouts of our teens.

What I'm trying to say, parents, is that while your teenager might treat you as his best friend, you must know how to balance your being a parent. The art of recognizing the need to keep distance or giving our teens a certain freedom is essential.

For instance, in coming up with decisions where a minor needs guidance on, such as which course to take up in college, you may get into the scene. But, in choosing which club to join, such as when your teen is more interested in swimming or karate club, don't force him to join the glee club.

When Ezekiel was in 8th Grade, his class was having a camp somewhere in a remote area in Metro Manila. It was then that the peace and order situation near the camp site was questionable where armed groups were reported to have been hiding nearby. I knew it based on Wilson's advice as per intelligence report.

Conversely, I was aware as well how important that camp was for Zekie because that should be his last camp with his classmates in his school since he and others would be transferring to different international schools after that school year.

Then came the day before said camp where I saw a letter clipped in my desk. It was a long letter from Zekie respectfully pleading for my permission with 101 explanations justifying his reasons. The letter ended up by telling me to not ever mention about the camp anymore if I would not allow him to join. Zekie also said that he would understand me whatever my decision would be; but, for sure he would be sad.

That particular situation was heartbreaking and challenging for me and Tsip as parents. We were very much empathetic towards our son, but, we were also concerned about the blatant risk if we would have him join the camp.

To cut the story short, we did not allow Ezekiel to join the camp. Despite that, our relationship was not severed.

In contrast, the year after that camp, Ezekiel had an opportunity for an Exchange Scholarship at La Mezia Terme in Italy, with side trip to Rome and Singapore. It was such a handsome birthday surprise for him that we allowed him to travel by himself and explore European education and culture as a teen.

Another year has passed and as our teen gets to acclimatize with his teenage life, we would allow him to hang out with friends more often. The other night, he sleptover with vacationing foreign friend along with two other former classmates from Mahatma Gandhi International School at Somerset Millenium Hotel in Makati. The day after, he hang out at The Ascott Hotel Makati with another group of friends from Victory Christian International School who traveled with him for the exchange scholarship in Italy last year.

The important thing is that the parents are aware of the company and whereabouts of their teens as well as of the safety and security of the place where they go. Set the limitations as well. For instance, what time you expect the teen to be home, and suchlike.

There is always a right time for everything. Our teens should know by heart about it.

1. ***Think his age, feel his age.*** As parents, be open-minded about how your teens feel. Try to understand where his actions, choices and decisions come from, considering the circumstances and his lack of experience. Talk to him properly

to explain issues.

Last week, my 15-year old opened up to me that his vacationing foreign friends who are former classmates are enticing him to go with them in Greenhills to get fake identification cards which they intend to present in clubs as the age limit for entrance is 18 years old and up. Thank goodness that my teen takes wisdom from us before doing anything.

I was very much stunned to hear that, of course, but am able to gracefully stretch out my understanding and composure. Honestly, I couldn't say a word for a few minutes, because I wasn't ready to hear those issues from my son. In fact, it took me days and series of casual talks to enlighten Zekie about that aspect. One time, as we were having lunch with my high school friends at TGI Friday's, we casually shared with Zekie our teenage and professional life escapades. And at another instance, I had my sister-in-law share her personal night life adventures as well. In all those, like a friend, I cautiously explained to my teen the repercussions of being with the wrong associates or making bad choices.

The point here is that as parents, it is incumbent for us to show that we care while showing a certain level of understanding and respect on our teen's choices.

Be reasonable! As we know, for instance, teenage is characterized by a period where your kids develop crushes. Normally, it is the time where puppy love or hero worship blooms. Don't stick your nose in whoever your minor admires. Let him develop his own sense of identity. Slyly give sound advice when needed, and set easy-to-understand rules, such as: "It's okay to have crush, but I trust that you won't get into any serious relationships, for now, because you're too young."

1. ***Being open makes you close.*** Have an accommodating atmosphere when dealing with your teenager. Initiate a

welcoming attitude by being open to him. For instance, talk to him how happy you were upon being commended for accomplishing your office tasks, saying what exactly your boss said. Talk about your interests, opinions on politics and vacation plans. If you would share personal thoughts to your minor, he would most likely, open up his own feelings in the same manner.

1. ***Let his voice be heard.*** Begin involving your teen in coming up with minor family decisions, such as how and where he would like the family to spend the next weekend.

Recently, when I was busy developing my "The Green Kitchen Gourmet Products," Zekie was with me in my meetings and researches. Along with conceptualizations were the collaterals, logo, brochures and branding requirements. In most of those, I asked for Zekie's suggestions and sincerely considered his youthful opinions since he's an unbiased consumer and he aspires to take up Business Studies in Senior High this year.

1. ***Proper orientation on sensitive issues starts from home.*** Teenagers usually face a bucketload of questions and difficulties as regards changes in many aspects of their lives. While the schools and the real world offer their own ways of teaching the minors, it's always safest and most ideal to learn from home. For instance, the menstrual cycle and basic hygiene are better explained by a mom to her teenage girl. Issues on sexuality or sexual awareness, drugs awareness, among others, are best explained at home as the parents inject moral values along the way in clarifying sensitive subjects.

Though the teenage period may be a critical stage for the child and the guiding parents, the same could also be an thrilling moment of discovery and learning for both parties. It may also be an excellent opportunity to promote a solid parent-child relationship, especially when you want to develop closeness in the family.

As a constant extension of the classroom, make your home a conducive place in nurturing and supporting the teen. With proper guidance from us parents, we are sure to lead our teens to the right way, as we properly prepare them for their life as adults.

Breaktime: Positivity Check

A person who recognizes the value of wisdom will never run out of it.—Kumander Misis

CHAPTER FOURTEEN

Wrestling Against One's Self

"I don't really understand myself, for I want to do what is right, but I don't do it. Instead, I do what I hate." This verse in Romans 7:15 bares an ironic truth about human nature.

How much do you know yourself?

Over and over again, we tend to do things we don't mean to do. Agreed? Blame it to life stressors, or midlife crisis, postpartum period, or perhaps, to menopausal or andropausal stage, mood swings, upbringing, temptations and so on— the list just gets longer and we are likely to deal with the same experience of struggling to do what is right.

Apostle Paul, the author of Romans was not exculpated from this experience and admitted that he, too, did not understand himself during his time. With this in mind, and as I share my personal testimony, I am optimistic that we would understand our personalities better and be heedful of the following realities:

1. ***You cannot lie to yourself.*** One day, my son Zecheriah (Strong) approached me and said: "Mom, my brother and I know how to determine whether a person is lying or not." Then I asked him how, where he said: "When a person is telling a lie, his pupils will grow big as he talks and the voice pitch of the person gets higher". He even demonstrated it by asking his brother Zekie to tell anything fallacious. As observed, Zekie's pupils grew big as he talked. A moment later, Zecheriah approached me again and said: "Mom, I looked at the mirror and told a lie to see if my pupils would grow big. I was surprised that it didn't work. So, it only means, we cannot lie to ourselves."

Yes, we can use all types of facades to project a certain image or emotion to the world, or even to deceive others, but we cannot lie to ourselves because we know the truth.

1. ***Area Unknown.*** Social media and blogging, more than a hobby, have turned out to be my personal ministry where I would share my thoughts, works and life experiences, on the hope to inspire others. Along the course, it is common that Facebook followers especially from other countries whom I am not personally acquainted with would always PM me to ask my age and often, whether I am single with kids or married with kids. Not to mention that most followers would send me inspiring messages telling me that they look up to me as a role model or that they love my writings or posts, and so forth.

Undeniably, people perceive each of us in different ways based on impressions. People, no matter how close to us, may see a certain part of us, but not all of us as a person.

At this stage of my life, I would occasionally and scrupulously ask myself whether I'm doing the right thing or not, or whether my thoughts and feelings towards different things are normal. The truth is I don't have 100% complete understanding of myself irrespective of my age, social status and profession. Fortunately, however, I was given a very tolerant husband who does not get tired of listening to me and understanding my concerns. Nevertheless, it does not guarantee that he will have an exact grasp of how I think or feel at all times, simply because we are two different individuals.

And that reminds me of Johari Window back in my AB Psychology years, where basically (1) there is that part of ourselves that we see and others see, (2) there are aspects that others see in us but we are not aware of (3) and there is our private/ secret space in ourselves, which we know but others do not know (4) and there is the most mysterious area in our own self which neither ourselves nor others see.

It resides in the unconscious or subconscious part of us—an area that only God knows.

3. ***When the Struggle Gets Tough, Be True.*** Now, we are settled to the fact that there are aspects in ourselves that we, too, do not know nor understand. Therefore, it is normal for each person to have some problematic ways and behavior that he might want to deal with, but in reality he is incapable of. Who, then, can deal with them?

Believe it or not, even King David with all his power, valor, riches, achievements and fame had the same challenging area in his person which he surrendered under God's command allowing God Himself to deal with it. In Psalm 139 David wrote:

v 23 Search me, O God, and know my heart!
Try me and know my thoughts!
v24 And see if there be any grievous way in me,
and lead me in the way everlasting!

The key to doing the good that we want to do and avoiding the fight against our own self is to change the way we think. The key to changing the way we think is by feeding our thoughts with holiness. And the key to holiness is through God's work alone. There's no other channel. If you would try to be holy by yourself, forget it! Lest you will definitely fail.

Philippians 4:8

Finally, brothers and sisters, whatever is true, whatever is noble, whatever is right, whatever is pure, whatever is lovely, whatever is admirable—if anything is excellent or praiseworthy—think about such things.

Ref: Psalm 139

1 O Lord, you have searched me and known me!
2 You know when I sit down and when I rise up;
you discern my thoughts from afar.
3 You search out my path and my lying down
and are acquainted with all my ways.

4 Even before a word is on my tongue,
behold, O Lord, you know it altogether.
5 You hem me in, behind and before,
and lay your hand upon me.
6 Such knowledge is too wonderful for me;
it is high; I cannot attain it.
7 Where shall I go from your Spirit?
Or where shall I flee from your presence?
8 If I ascend to heaven, you are there!
If I make my bed in Sheol, you are there!
9 If I take the wings of the morning
and dwell in the uttermost parts of the sea,
10 even there your hand shall lead me,
and your right hand shall hold me.
11 If I say, "Surely the darkness shall cover me,
and the light about me be night,"
12 even the darkness is not dark to you;
the night is bright as the day,
for darkness is as light with you.
13 For you formed my inward parts;
you knitted me together in my mother's womb.
14 I praise you, for I am fearfully and wonderfully made.[a]
Wonderful are your works;
my soul knows it very well.
15 My frame was not hidden from you,
when I was being made in secret,
intricately woven in the depths of the earth.
16 Your eyes saw my unformed substance;
in your book were written, every one of them,
the days that were formed for me,
when as yet there was none of them.
17 How precious to me are your thoughts, O God!

How vast is the sum of them!
18 If I would count them, they are more than the sand.
I awake, and I am still with you.
19 Oh that you would slay the wicked, O God!
O men of blood, depart from me!
20 They speak against you with malicious intent;
your enemies take your name in vain.[b]
21 Do I not hate those who hate you, O Lord?
And do I not loathe those who rise up against you?
22 I hate them with complete hatred;
I count them my enemies.
23 Search me, O God, and know my heart!
Try me and know my thoughts!
24 And see if there be any grievous way in me,
and lead me in the way everlasting!

1. ***Tears is a Language the Lord Understands.*** Close family and friends have a strong impression that I am a very tough person as that's what they tell me. Without them knowing, behind this strength, many times in my life, I was also attacked by uncertainties, guilt, trauma, confusion, weakness, questions, and qualms where I sensed I couldn't even utter the right words to pray for. Looking back, I was actually numb during those times and the only armament I had were my tears, transparently defending my case through my frailty. Like a helpless baby who couldn't talk, waiting for the mother to cuddle her.

In all those occasions, I felt how the power of God worked most, enabling me to overcome everything that came my way; and with each circumstance, I witnessed miracles before my very eyes as I reap blessings after blessings. [Details will be in my books "*PROOF* (beyond reasonable doubt)" and "*POWER OF GRATEFULNESS*" to be published soon].

In the New Testament, we would recall Mary the sister of Lazarus who knelt at Jesus' feet. She was crying and began to wash the back of the Lord's feet with her tears and dried them with her hair. Then she kissed our Lord's feet over and over again, anointing them constantly with perfume.

Nobody knew what exactly the woman was thinking. But she caught the Lord's attention that He turned towards her.

Luke 7:44 says:

"*Then he turned toward the woman and said to Simon, "Do you see this woman? I came into your house. You did not give me any water for my feet, but she wet my feet with her tears and wiped them with her hair.*"

Shedding tears is not a male or a female thing, nor is a sign of cowardice. When we cry to the Lord, we humble down ourselves before Him, acknowledging our need of Him and allowing Him to take control of the situation we are into.

1. ***Let Go and Let God.*** As a final word, in times that we wrestle against ourselves and our very nature, relax and give the battle to God. Remember:

God knows you and you are beautiful in His eyes.

"For you formed my inward parts; you knitted me together in my mother's womb. I praise you, for I am fearfully and wonderfully made." Psalm 139:13-14

God's thoughts are higher than your thoughts. Stop the brain strain!

"For my thoughts are not your thoughts, neither are your ways my ways, declares the LORD. For as the heavens are higher than the earth, so are my ways higher than your ways and my thoughts than your thoughts." Isaiah 55:9

God is able to carry our burdens and promises to give us rest.

"Come to me, all you who are weary and burdened, and I will give you rest." Matthew 11:28.

Not that I have already obtained all this, or have already arrived at my goal, but I press on to take hold of that for which Christ Jesus took hold of me. Philippians 3:12

CHAPTER FIFTEEN

Dating Ideas to Married Christian Couples

Following the footsteps of my parents who, by the way, have just celebrated their 45th wedding anniversary this month, Tsip and I go on constant dating, so as to preserve our marriage bond. And it works! We feel we get closer and happier each day without the so-called closeness fatigue.

While you might think that a Christian couple's dating has to feel and look somewhat religious like going to the church and attending prayer meetings, on the contrary, a married Christian couple's dating can be a thrilling experience that creates closeness to the husband and wife.

Should you be curious on how we set exciting dates, here are some ideas, which I hope you'll try, too:

Dating at home.

As a busy couple, sometimes, we need to buy time by never having to leave our home.

Attention, guys! If cooking for your wife is unusual, why not cook for your wife this time. Set the table in a romantic arrangement, just like how it is in a fine dining restaurant. Since you know your wife's favorite food, take an effort to cook a simple menu that is made special with love. Present it the way a gourmet chef would. Complete the cozy atmosphere by lighting candles on a dim dining area. Play a classical or jazz music on the background. That's simply romantic, isn't it? By the way, wives can do the same for their husband.

Breakfast in bed. What a nice morning it is for a wife to wake up with freshly picked flowers beside her, and a matching sweet note that says: "Breakfast is ready. I hope you'll like it." Prepare a breakfast-in-bed set and put it in a tray. Lay it down on the bed or on a table in the bedroom. Make the breakfast set look special by adding fresh fruit or salad sidings for more color.

To help you think, here are some breakfast ideas:

Tropical Breakfast

Waffles or French Toast

Bagel Breakfast

At home, my personal preference is English Breakfast—English muffin, eggs, and orange juice and brewed coffee.

Tsip is good at many things except for cooking. That's why, he takes effort to compensate the same by constantly bringing "to-go" food for me. Sometimes, it's just as simple as "Starbucks coffee" or Pinoy snacks like "ginataan" sent on ordinary afternoons through his staff.

Movie time. Spend a comfortable night with your husband either in the bedroom or in the living room as you watch a good movie. Prepare movie time snacks and hot or cold beverages that you would both enjoy. Re-arrange your mock theater in such a way that would make it look special.

Just to share a bit more, last Valentine's day, I even printed a replica theater pass and gave my husband, and our two kids their own tickets, with corresponding seat number and free popcorn and meal stub. It was a lot of fun.

Picnic at the backyard. The next suggestion is a classic in our home. If you have a home garden, invite your spouse on a pre-arranged picnic with your kids, family or close friends in your own backyard. Make the occasion unique by making a personalized invitation for your spouse, and have her dress up just like she would in a real picnic. Prepare couples' games to make the moment more entertaining.

Explore new places. If you have extra budget, it would be nice to explore local or international places together which you haven't been to, and create memorable sweet moments in those places. Consider to be out in the sun. Try nature tripping, such as hiking, canoe ride, biking, and joy riding. Cruising opportunity is such a treat. Check out your local travel agencies for special deals. I personally preserve these memorable moments through photos and blogging.

That reminds me of a lovely couple where the wife is in her 50s and the husband is in late 60s. They would post up on social media, almost every single day, their travel and "we time" moments. It's inspiring seeing love and romance on news feeds. Romance should be an uninterrupted routine in married life!

Restaurant hopping. For a change, try going to different restaurants serving fusion cuisines and enjoy the food together. It would be cool to have a casual or serious talk about your short-term and long-term plans in a dinner date. It's equally fine to simply have fun reviewing the menu and services of a restaurant. I often do this inadvertently and effortlessly. The next thing is that I find myself writing something on Trip Advisor.

Couple's Spa. Relieving stress may be done together! Have a regular relaxing moment with your spouse by going to health clubs or spa. In Manila, we opt to call a masseuse for home service, especially when it's late to visit a good spa.

Group dating. To avoid monotony, set a group couples' date with friends and associates who have similar Christian family values as yours. It's a good way to strengthen your ties with your spouse. Our church Day by Day Christian Ministries arranges retreat and various special activities intended for couples. I think, organized activities like those are helpful.

As married Christian couples, let your love grow each day and establish wonderful marital friendship along the way by dating regularly.

CHAPTER SIXTEEN

Dozen Secrets to Enjoy your Work

If there be any extraordinary trait that I admire most about Tsip, it is his unmatched commitment towards his work. I've mentioned in the earlier chapter of this book how as a neophyte officer, he was very much committed and dedicated to his tasks.

To this date, he has been carrying on the same attitude anywhere he is assigned.

Is coming to work a struggle to you? Do you feel you're dealing with unlikable personalities?

For sure, just like me, we have all been meeting unaccommodating and difficult-to-deal-with personalities everywhere trying to make simple things unnecessarily laborious.

For instance, you will just need to secure an ID or passport or TOR, and suchlike, or you need someone's approval on something, she or he tends to make things hard for you. Hence, it's either we extend our patience to understand her –giving our own justifications, such as, "Maybe she's deprived or problematic, that's why she hates the world" – or, we let our undomesticated boldness come out.

In all cases, I noticed that being rude, brusque and arrogant make these unfriendly people treat you better. Should it be that way all the time? Should we have to utter vile curses and threats upon someone just to be treated well?

In truth, it gives us more benefits being nice to people. That light feeling of bliss whenever we extend help and goodness to someone is fulfilling.

Some other reasons I see why one doesn't enjoy work are: loads of responsibilities with deadlines, fatigue, low pay, unsatisfactory working environment, long hours of inconvenient travel, and so on. Whew! That's exhausting.

From my Linked In account, a Dale Carnegie training consultant and enthusiasm expert asked: "What is that one quality that is essential in all aspects of life?" The thread had run for a long time, and various opinions arise up to this very minute.

Why do you think so? It's because different people think differently and each of them would like to share his own views.

The point is, in all phases of life, such as in our work, happiness is how we personally define it. Not because you're a CEO, you are sure to be happy. Or not because you're at the entry level in an organization, you are unhappy.

As I write this book today, I checked on my word count and didn't notice that I'm now on my 29,864th word. My excitement and passion do not diminish. I simply love what I'm doing!

My range of exposures to different working environments locally, internationally, online and offline allowed me to come about with tips to enjoy work based on my experience, such as these twelve as listed below:

1. *Be thankful about your work each day, and look forward to another day.*

1. *Have an optimistic attitude towards your boss and colleagues.* No negative vibes, please. No badmouthing, as well.

1. *Be an encourager than a critic.*

1. *Do not be a burden or create any burden in your organization.*

1. *Have a CAN DO IT attitude.* Subordinates: Obey first before you explain. (I didn't mean before you complain!)

1. *Bad: Don't THINK you're better than your boss; he won't be in his position for nothing.*

Worse: Don't SAY you're better than your boss. (unless you wish to lose your job!)

1. *Boss or superiors: Don't think your men are idiot, moron or stupid. Trust them. Reward them, too, and recognize their talents.*

1. *Be a continuous learner.* Complacency is dangerous.

1. *Stop that crab mentality.* Be happy with one's achievements and accomplishments.

1. *Be open to and consider suggestions and criticisms.*

1. *Adjust to your environment; life will be less complicated.* One common mistake is that we tend to change our environment in favor of us. Technically, that's fine, but be sure you're ready to face conflicts.

1. *Be a good virus!* —In other words, be contagious in a positive way.

Let's all enjoy our work, and in turn, make others enjoy working with us!

Breaktime: Positivity Check

12 April 2017— I had to interrupt my sons' movie time together at Zekie's room for a precious 12 o'clock moment. Zekie turned 16 today! Happy birthday!

We had a short ice cream break, plus sermon from the parents hahah! (seriously, guidance on teenage life and future career) and thanksgiving prayer afterwards. With all the blessings we've experienced and received through our sons from their birth, what else can we ask for?

If I may, let me share some of the wisdom I shared with the birthday boy. I told him that for me, happiness is a decision (I decide to be happy, and so I am!)...Fulfillment is a mental and emotional state uninfluenced by external forces (I feel fulfilled with respect to my own standards without comparing my life with anybody else's life), and success is how we personally define it, not by anyone else. Set goals, be proactive. That is to have plan b, c to z in case your expectations don't happen without your control. And you will be unshaken whatever happens.

Happiness, fulfillment and success—all these when enjoyed in this life are gifts from Above. I understand that Zekie might have his own set of principles in the future... but, certainly, the values we've practiced in this family will forever be in his heart.

"Train up a child in the way he should go, and when he is old he will not depart from it." (Proverbs 22:6)

CHAPTER SEVENTEEN

PNP Behind the Lens: Compassionate Law Enforcement

Today, let's make a time travel to about eight years ago when Tsip was then Major Doromal and was assigned at Provincial Regional Office 4A (PRO4A) of the Highway Patrol Group, known as the CALABARZON area covering Cavite, Laguna, Batangas, Rizal and Quezon provinces.

Tsip was then the Provincial Chief of Laguna and, of course, family time was of essence. Thanks to my old blog that I got to document this:

So, it was a Saturday night, my two kids, my husband... they're all snoozing. My husband fell sound asleep while playing with our kids. Understandable enough because he just came from a whole day of blood-letting activity in Cavite.

Next, I got my digicam to transfer my school photos taken this week in my Education class. Until an hour had passed without realizing that I got so steeped at browsing the hundreds of photos stored in our digicam. Most of those retained are my husband's activities in the Region Region 4A as the Philippine National Police Highway Patrol Group Provincial Chief of Laguna.

Green revolution, bloodletting, three-day ride for a cause, tree planting in CALABARZON (Provinces of Cavite, Laguna, Batangas, Rizal, Quezon), school supplies distribution for kids in remote areas, rescue missions, feeding activities, help for typhoon victims, medical missions, road safety seminars, and a lot more— all these are documented in our digicam. Activities which are not necessarily part of the job of police officers.

Interestingly, I see hundreds, and sometimes, about two thousand volunteers happily participating on projects.

Contemplating on the photos, I told myself: "These Police Officers are doing a great job for communities. They are enormous influences and influencers of the nation as shown by the people's active support and volunteerism on projects done on the regional level."

"Compassionate Law Enforcement!" –a phrase precisely descriptive of what these police officers do. This expression I involuntarily uttered and coined tonight as I'm so stirred just by looking at the photos. Opportune for today's call for national transformation and at the point in time where police officers, in general, are being dreaded upon by the commoners due to negative feedbacks everywhere.

Again, there is such thing as Compassionate Law Enforcement. In fact, there's a great deal of uniformed men and women doing the same endeavor but unknown to most of us. And so, pardon me if I am inclined towards PCI Wilson Doromal's accomplishments on this writing. He's my husband, anyway. But I keep in mind, Law of Power Number One: "*Do not outshine the master*". Thus, I give credit to PNP HPG4A Regional Chief Col. Gardiola (who at the present time is Gen. Gardiola, Director of the Highway Patrol Group) whose leadership and heart for the people are unsurpassed.

Mabuhay, PNP HPG4A and HGP4A Force Multipliers who always have vigorous cooperation for the success of laudable programs as mentioned above!

While it is difficult to give what we treasure most, it is more difficult to give what we don't have. But the most difficult of all is to beg from somebody else something that we need. So, it's always best to share what we have.

Finally, my fervent hope is that the virus of compassion may be dispersed in all the branches of the government, even in the corporate world, in small industries, in the different sectors of society, in barangays and in our homes through efforts like those mentioned.

After all, perfection is attained only when something is begun. There can be no victory without daring attempts.

Just a few more side notes, please.

As a social entrepreneur and an artistic and green revolutionist, I'm very grateful that I was given a husband who has the same goals as mine. Even back when m Tsip was assigned at the Manila Police District, he demonstrated credence in the supremacy of unity among different sectors of society. When he was Precinct Commander of Gagalangin, Station 1, he formed GISPO or Gagalangin Integrated Sectors for Peace and Order; and when he was the Precinct Commander of Lawton, Station 5, he founded Ayala-Taft Anti-Crime Consortium, both of which had been dynamic partners of the Local Police in peace enforcement and successful capture of criminals.

Breaktime: Positivity Check

While it is difficult to give what we treasure most, it is more difficult to give what we don't have. But the most difficult of all is to beg from somebody else something that we need. So, it's always best to share what we have. – Kumander Misis

CHAPTER EIGHTEEN

Leave the Crab Behind

There's this comical police officer who has the habit of telling negative stories about almost all of his previous superiors and workmates. He seems to feel unhappy about any achievement by fellow officers.

Any attempt to ask his feedback about anyone, expect a destructive input from this officer. In his eyes, he's the sole capable officer in any assignment. Then came, one day, a serious instance where said officer needed help from one of those whom he spoke against in the past. Sadly, he failed to get any favor from that person he badmouthed about.

An achievement, whether gigantic or undersized, adds to one's self-gratification, offers some sort of self-actualization and usually drives a person to aspire for more, or reach for better goals.

Achievement equals inner pride, and pride entails pleasure on the part of the achiever. Self-actualization is a human need; accordingly, it is normal to be happy and proud about our achievements or accomplishments. For sure, Abraham Maslow, Kurt Goldstein, Carl Rogers and some other pillars of human psychology would agree with it.

How happy are you at observing others achieve their goals? How do you feel seeing people flourish in their endeavors? Do you appreciate the accomplishments of people around you? Are you glad with someone else's success?

Whether we accept it or not, if we self-assess today and think that we actually or secretly feel bad about seeing lovely things happening to people, chances are, we are guilty of the loathsome trait of crab mentality!

I did research online on the concept and roots of crab mentality and it is so disgusting that "crab mentality" is often associated with

Filipinos worldwide. This metaphor is believed to have been derived from a phenomenon which occurs in a bucket of crabs. If any crab attempts to flee from a bucket of live crabs, the other crabs will pull it back down and will not allow the co-crab to escape. Occasionally, the crabs seem almost nasty, waiting until the fellow crab has almost escaped before tugging it back into the bucket.

Have you experienced situations where people whom you trust most pull you down, silently or blatantly? He could be a friend, a best friend, a neighbor, a relative, an officemate or a family member... and at PNP or AFP, sometimes, your very own classmates.

Was there an instance in your life calling for a celebration –as when you passed the board exams, got a promotion, appointed to an office, offered a high salary, received an award, discovered the Philippines (kidding), or won in the lottery — and someone obviously pretended to ignore such fact or deliberately took no notice of the festivity? Instead, he thought of unconstructive junks to divert people's attention to intrigues unrelated to the issue at hand? Congratulations, you have just been a certified victim of crab mentality!

The term "crab mentality" is used to describe a category of selfish attitude which literally means, "if I can't have it, neither can you." While this term is widely used generally among Filipinos, I believe, this is prevalent among any other nationalities in the world. Take for example the racists who could not admit that our professionals are more clever than their people. (This is not to generalize everyone, of course!) They simply hire Filipino workers in their country but do not admit the ingenuity of Filipino talents. Oh, well, perhaps in the real world, Filipino is the lone breed who had the nerve and honesty to vocally admit that he has this trait, that's why crab mentality is often linked on Filipinos.

Crab mentality is in the air, domestically and globally.

In the government, when one refuses to support certain initiatives by the leaders of the opposing party or political rival, in a way, the same ultimately drags the whole country down. That is crab mentality.

In office environments, crab mentality can be predominantly upsetting when officemates criticize each other, rather than pass on good wishes to someone who earns a commendation.

Indeed, a simple label of having crab mentality is a pitiable reflection of one's character whether you are a Filipino or not. It is rooted out of envy and false pride and could strike at all levels of life. From our workplace, to our community, to our homes, to the government, in private institutions, in churches and in any organization... it lingers.

Leave the crab behind! The key here is that you self-diagnose that you have it, and decide to abandon it totally for good.

If by now you have identified the crabs around you, keep distance from them without being uncivil. However, when you feel that you are the crab in your setting, recognize such fact and transform.

CHAPTER NINETEEN

Summertime Ironies are Cool

Truly, human life is full of absurdities. Often, the more that we treat a person well, the more he tends to abuse us.

Have you noticed that people, in general, give more expensive gifts to the well-to-do than to the ones who need material gifts desperately? Or sometimes we would ask: "Why are the bad ones more moneyed or lucky, and the kind-hearted ones suffer a lot?"

Don't think extensively. It's technically like drinking a cup of hot coffee in summertime.

Working online has been an electrifying avenue for learning on my part.

For instance, through extensive reading, it was an enormous surprise when I learned that there are people who actually dread things which are unnecessarily scary at all for most of us. Check this out:

Believe it or not, there are those who fear color white (leukophobia). Or, there is such thing as fear of China/ Chinese (Sinophobia), of computers (computerphobia), of decision-making (decidophobia), of wealth (plutophobia), of writing (graphophobia), of dolls and children (pedophobia), or of number 8 (octophobia) and even of the word or color yellow (xanthophobia).

Ironic for some, but this is reality.

When my son Strong was in first grade, he was intentionally pushed hard by a female foreign classmate when they were walking by the school corridor. I knew it was planned because Strong was silently seated beside me at that time when two foreign schoolmates fetched him, a Canadian and an Israeli. In about thirty seconds from leaving my place, I heard my little Strong crying already. I felt really bad seeing that he bumped his lips on the wall.

Right then and there, at the top of my voice, I told my son to fight back and defend himself. Ironically, the pitiable boy, with his limited vocabulary, and while crying said: "But Mom, we are not allowed. That's not good."

It was a fresh traumatic experience for my younger of two sons since he's new in the school. He skipped kinder and was accelerated to Grade One when he was admitted as full scholar that school year at Mahatma Gandhi International School.

As soon as we got home, Strong animatedly shared the bullying incident with his Dad. And of course I was expecting to hear a sound protective parental advice, but Tsip had taken the story differently. He said, "That's fine Strong. As long as you're doing the right thing and do not mistreat others, you will be alright. You will be blessed because of your kindness."

Ironic for a typical policeman, isn't it?.

From outside of the Philippines, a lot of critics opine that the Filipinos are blindly tolerant about the supposed extra-judicial killings in the country. They find it ironic to be supporting someone whom they perceive as a mass killer president.

Whereas that's the opposing conception by anti-Duterte groups, in the eyes of the President's supporters, it is improper and ironic for the critics to perceive the whole situation as linked on President Duterte's orders since the latter is known to be just and knowledgeable of the laws.

Seeing similar arguments and news recently, I felt like it's a good time to write about ironies of life.

As early as now, for instance, many of us are already worried about the inaccessibility of public transport on Holy Week. Every year, people are apt to stop from work from Maundy Thurday through Black Saturday in observance of the passion and death of Christ.

I'm not sure about how it is in other Christian countries. In the Philippines, the feeling of how the regular day-to-day activities of people are likely to slow down a bit during the Holy Week is quite perceptible. Expectedly, there will be less available PUVs from Maundy Thursday through Saturday during the Holy Week, although Grab and Uber will surely keep up with their operation.

Personally, as a Christian, rather than observing Holy Week in deep sorrow, I believe that it has to be a moment of festivities. When Jesus said "it is finished" (John 19:30), the saving grace of God had been fulfilled and was bestowed upon mankind finally, once and for all.

The greatest ironies of all generations, I suppose, are stated in Bible as in 1 Peter 3: 18 and suchlike:

"For Christ died for sins once for all, the righteous for the unrighteous, to bring you to God. He was put to death in the body but made alive by the Spirit".

As you can see, this is where a righteous (Christ) absorbed the unrighteousness of the world and where bodily death was transformed into life.

Another irony is stated in Romans 6:23 where it says, *"for the wages of sin is death; but the gift of God is eternal life through Jesus Christ our Lord".*

Please take a look at this irony: we are supposed to die because we are sinful, but God offered us life through Jesus Christ.

Knowing in faith that Jesus died for me and that He rose from the dead and that I will be living with Him in eternity is a great reason for ultimate celebration. It is truly astounding that whenever we observe Holy Week in the country, we would fill the air with melancholy, thinking that the Lord Jesus is still in the state of suffering or hanging dead on the cross.

Don't get me wrong, please. It is not that I am being religious or something. Neither do I have any intention to infringe on anybody else's faith. My contention is that having the chance to work online and publish e-books put me into the best position and grant me a perfect avenue to share my thoughts, based on facts and researches, to the widest possible reach and in just one click.

Now, applying this principle and based on facts which I gathered online, I learned that unlike before, the word "God" is not anymore included in the list of most searched words. Though "sex" or "porn" remains on top 500. Interesting, isn't it? The millennials of www seems to be no longer in search of God.

I anticipate that this writing would emerge as a sincere effort of communicating to the readers that there is God and the one orchestrating our life in such a lovely way is the kind of God whom Christians like me have faith in.

As a final point, I would like to leave you this irony from John 11:25-26 (NIV): "Jesus said , *I am the resurrection and the life. He who believes in me will live, even though he dies; and whoever lives and believes in me will never die.* "

Have a divine week and a fulfilled life, everyone.

CHAPTER TWENTY

On Sowing and Reaping

Tsip and I have been together in many real storms and life storms already for the past seventeen years of marriage. In most of those heavy typhoons, he was assigned in the provinces.

One time, a mega typhoon came and I was alone in our condominium taking care of my little kids Strong and Zekie.

At the height of Typhoon Falcon where the deafening rainfall was hitting the ground and the roofs so hardly, I heard my son Zecheriah yelling as he pulled the curtain and peeped by the window to see what was going on outside: *"Lord, don't make us die. Just keep us healthy. Don't make us afraid. Stop the rain right now. Stop the rain right now!"*

As my innocent 5-year old was repeatedly saying "stop the rain right now," he shouted even louder. He caught my attention and so, I paused from my work, watched him as I smiled in silence and asked the boy what he was doing. *"I'm praying so that the rain will stop and we don't die,"* Zecheriah answered at the top of his voice.

I knew my son was afraid that's why he was praying. But beyond that, I realized, too, that I and my husband had sown seeds of faith in our kids' lives, hence they reap the amount of faith in proportion to their current situation, age and level.

Sowing and reaping is science. "*Sowing*", literally, is the science of producing life (as in plants) and by "*reaping*", life is preserved (where human eats the harvest).

About seven years ago, I was able to grab a copy of the film "The Secret" by Rhonda Byrne from a friend. The film explained how the optimistic principle of the Law of Attraction affects our lives and had affected the lives of all the great achievers, great leaders and great minds in history like Beethoven, Lincoln, Emerson, Edison and Einstein who knew about it. The Law of Attraction is tantamount to reaping what you sow in your mind. If you sow success, you will reap success. If we do not care for the environment, we will suffer from pollution. If you think of beautiful things, beautiful things will happen to you.

I realized that the thing called "The Secret" is knowing who you really are. Thus, in every aspect of life, it's up to me whether to "aspire" or simply "command." Things will happen as how I perceive them. The rationale is that as a Christian, I am a princess, my Father is a King!

The Bible says "*Be not deceived; God is not mocked: for whatsoever a man soweth, that shall he also reap*" *Galatians 6:7*. Also, "*...those who plow evil and those who sow trouble reap it.*"

Job 4:8 Furthermore, it says; "*...he that sows sparingly will also reap sparingly; and he that sows bountifully will also reap bountifully*" *2 Corinthians 9:6*

In my younger years, I used to read inspirational books by Dr. Norman Vincent Peale where the positive principles in life were being taught. From then on, I became more aggressive thinking that everything is possible as long as I believe. I lived by it! I mean, "certainly it works!"

Sometimes, we tend to ask when objectionable things happen in our lives: "Is this the fruit of my hardwork?" or "Is this what I get from my goodness or faithfulness?" Better think again.

Yes, we might have sown good seeds. But are we sure it is the time for harvest? Harvest season comes in God's time alone. If we force to harvest at our own time, we might later on complain of harvesting stunted or underdeveloped fruit.

Time is ours to enjoy, but timing has to be left to the will of the Almighty.

There are loads of circumstances in our lives daily where our character and attitudes are being tested. Along the way, we tend to sow the seeds of envy, greed, injustice, worry, anger, discouragement, anxiety, depression, rebellion, indolence, among others. At the end of the day, we question ourselves why our life is mixed-up or gloomy.

Keep in mind that what we sow is what we reap, and it is not me who said it.

Rather than being perceived as a mere theory, it is, in fact, a universal principle and the effects of which will automatically transpire in our lives. It is as certain as water will boil at 100 degrees Celsius.

What do you really want to happen in your family, career, business or personal life today?

Whatever you desire: conceptualize, visualize, actualize, realize and recognize.

In the country, we are generally being discouraged to give anything to street kids or beggars asking for money. The reason, they say, is to prevent the proliferation of syndicates using kids or the elderly as a means of artful extortion of money from the naïve public.

There is someone I know who has been consistently giving help to the street kids even if it is not being tolerated by the government. Her reason is that although there is a possibility that the beggars knocking on our cars are bogus, we are not sure of the fact. She said, "unless you are certain that the same is a modus operandi by bad elements, help." When a person comes to you and you have the capacity to help, grab the opportunity and take action.

There came instances recently in this person's life where she needed help. She wanted to send her son to a good remote private school that she couldn't afford. Just before the start of the school year, she received a partial scholarship offer from a friend for her son without even applying for it, with all the terms she wanted.

On another occasion, the woman got into the midst of losing her job for an inevitable reason. Just before it happened, she received a call from a relative saying that her regular monthly commission for a marketing referral (something she was never aware of) would start that month. After that, she received three more job offers, giving her an opportunity to earn regular monthly income while doing what she loves doing at her own time.

Just like that woman in my anecdote, I could attest as to how the habit of sowing good seeds has been benefiting me in various unexpected ways.

Inspired by such occasions, I came to formulate this adage which I would like to leave you: " Even if life seems unfair, keep on doing what is good, right and just– properly or improperly , appropriately or inappropriately , with or without anyone seeing you. Certainly, in times you especially need them most, justice, righteousness and goodness you rendered will come back to you — properly, appropriately, miraculously and timely."

Breaktime: Positivity Check

Whatever you desire: conceptualize, visualize, actualize, realize and recognize.- Kumander Misis

Parallel Notes:

Parable of the Pechay as posted on Facebook version of Tales of Kumander Misis. I was deleting shots stored in my phone to free up some space when I came across a photo where I was standing beside my pechay plants. Incidentally, the plantbox is intended for my basil; however, just recently, my herbs dried up and perished. As regards these pakchoi or Chinese cabbage , last week during our family reflection, I shared my insights through this illustration: "We must be aware that everything changes—situations, life conditions, our leaders, the weather, the economy, emotions, our physique, etcetera. And though change comes and may happen constantly in this world, we should adapt to it and take it as an opportunity to shine, to come up with something productive or something good or even something better. Just like the drying up of our basil plants, for instance, instead of feeling disgruntled about it, we took it as an opportunity to utilize the space by sowing pechay #seeds. And now, the seeds have sprung out into beautiful veggies."

CHAPTER TWENTY- ONE

Teacher Mom in an Alternative Classroom

Now that I'm in my early 40's already, I'm at the point of realization that I was born to "learn, teach, lead, serve, minister and inspire". Note that those items should not be taken as separate from one another. Hence, my ultimate purpose as designed by our Almighty Creator is packaged as one into: "Learning, teaching, leading, serving, ministering and inspiring" in everything that I do. May it be in my capacity as a mother, as a wife, as a writer, as a speaker, as a friend or as a stranger.

My being a professional and licensed teacher is not the onset of my passion for teaching. As early as my elementary years at Santa Isabel College, I used to teach classes whenever I took charge as substitute student teacher when the teachers had meetings. In the church, I taught Sunday School starting on my 5th Grade.

Even then, I've always been an advocate of progressive education without me even knowing the exact term "progressive education." My natural learning and teaching style hasn't been traditional.

I recognize the fact that learning is not confined within the walls and corners of the classroom. Our homes, the world we step on are extensions of the classroom. I also practice eclectic strategies of teaching, from hands-on or experiential to the use of creative and theater arts, experimentation, and so on.

When Zecheriah was a toddler, he used to recite and re-enact all episodes of Spongebob with his brother Zekie who is four years older than he is. They would even exchange characters. It was entertaining to watch them throwing the full lines of each character, with all the cute expressions and intonations.

Strong also got to memorize long declamation pieces which he only heard during Zekie's few rehearsals at home. Prior to schooling, at about the age of 3, Strong already had a certain level of computing and internet savoir-faire. Everything that his brother did, he learned, too. He's also a self-taught taught swimmer. Even before he could swim, I saw how he was brave enough to dive into the swimming pool several times, and dove down to deeper water after a few minutes and swam.

From then to present our progressive education style has been doing well for us.

When Strong turned five, he had been consistently telling me that he did not want to go to school on the pretext that I was his teacher.

My dilemma then revolved around whether to send Strong to a real school or, "was it more sensible to enroll him to remote education program or homeschool curriculum?" With his style of learning, I wasn't sure if traditional school would be good for him. For that reason, I had such a fervent search for a progressive school where the program would fit with Strong's learning style.

Just at the right time, the boy was admitted to a prestigious international school where he got accelerated from kinder to first grade as he could already read and write before he started schooling. He also enjoyed full scholarship for five straight years. And the rest is history.

Did you know that there are good homeschools in the Philippines offering remote education programs?

There are those which would even register your child in a private school in the U.S.A. wherein at the convenience of your own home, the child will receive an official U.S. transcript. Transcripts from these accredited American schools may be used later on to enroll in the Philippines, U.S. and regular schools of other countries.

Some of the highlights of these homeschools are: (1) lessons, tests and grades are done by the parent/s or tutor (2) self-study at the child and teacher-parent's own pace (3) relaxed learning approach (4) Open time limit to finish a level (5) Subjects are based on student's interests (6) Bully-free, peer-pressure-free.

In the succeeding chapters of this book, I will share with you the perks we experience and enjoy in our progressive education and multiple intelligences advocacies.

Kumander Misis' Teaching Philosophy

In general, I dub my personal teaching philosophy "*altruistic passion in education*" wherein understanding the learner is the key. In effecting this philosophy, the teacher has to be extra empathetic and sensitive on the condition and needs of her students and be able to patiently and strategically reconcile these factors with her goals for the class and for each student.

I practice eclectic strategies of teaching in my classes—as well as at home in my capacity as educator mom—and ascertain that the student's interests are not only enhanced and stirred, more importantly, potentials are also introduced and discovered, recognizing individual differences and strengths. As regards this sphere, I encourage the employment of creativity, performing arts, experimentation, external exposures, technology, experiential and collaborative learning, and freedom of expression and inquiry in the class while giving everyone a balanced opportunity to shine.

It is my conviction that teachers are role models of the students and are vital conduits of moral and character formation of the learner; hence, irrespective of the subject area one teaches, values should be integrated.

I believe that classroom experience is a two-way process wherein teachers and students mutually teach and learn from each other. The places we go to are extensions of the classroom.

Learning is an endless process as long as one is willing to absorb knowledge. Considering this in mind, it is my job as a good teacher to think of and utilize appropriate motivational strategies to establish the student's positive learning attitude.

Finally, family support is, at all times, encouraged. I believe that teaching and learning begin at home and experience yields wisdom.

Fellow Anxious Parents

So much about those alien-sounding blah-blahs, I've had the chance in the past to talk to similarly anxious parents who, for security reasons, worry about the safety of their kids in school. We exchanged views and came up with diverse, and occasionally, humorous proposals.

One mom said she was contemplating on establishing her own pre-school in their home so as to ensure the safety of her kid. From that exchange of thoughts, this woman established her own progressive school right away. Today, that parent is still operating her own school. It's been successful. And that mom is currently in partnership with me as we plan to establish additional two more branches of her progressive school.

I know of another well-to-do family who chose to emigrate from the Philippines to settle in an inconspicuous Canadian territory. The mom opined that the best she could give her kids while in the Philippines was to send them to the best schools like Ateneo or international schools. Still, she was too much worried about her boys' future. I could still remember the seriousness of that mom's face when she said that her husband had to travel the world and research for a serene place with limited number of people (hence, with zero crime rate) and with vast space for potential development.

Okay, that's them. Let's talk about us– parents with simpler lifestyles. Do we have any better options? Every mother with little kids expresses the same thing. She wanted to be assured that her money spent on tuition fees will not go to waste. The next question should be: "How to Choose the Right School for your Child?"

How to Choose the Right School for Your Child

Due to curriculum changes locally (K-12), as well as in the international school where my children were studying (from IB to IGCSE concentration for secondary), I immediately looked at the possibility of transferring my kids to a local school for school year 2015-2016. Other than that, we had to move to a new home at that time.

As educator-mom, the same was a serious matter that I had to give attention to. And so, I planned proactively a year ahead.

To tell you, I read all the websites and reviews of as many good schools as I could find. They're really very helpful. Thank you everyone for blogging and reviewing! I also emailed and visited some of my choices, and that was the season where I realized that choosing the best school for your child is such a tactful process. For everyone's guidance, I wrote this Mommy's guide for parents like me:

Make a thorough research. List down your top 5, and then trim down your list to top 3. In doing so, consider your priorities. Your standards all depend on your preference.

Ask yourself yourself which aspects you give more weight into, e.g. (1) academics (2) reputation and/ or standing of the school— Do you prefer one that is among the top schools? Or does it really matter to you whether it is an old school or a pioneering school? (2) religious or non-sectarian (3) exclusive or co-ed (4) curriculum—international, local or both or whether traditional or progressive (5) crowd and environment— I had a hard time to decide on this. Should I go for a big school with many students or one with less number of students per class? Is the environment safe and peaceful? Are you happy to send your child to a school in a more crowded area such as those in the University Belt area? (6) Facilities—Basic or one with huge classrooms, with gymnasium, swimming pool, etc. (7) Discipline—I have read interesting reviews about good Catholic schools training their well-to-do students to be simple, where even branded socks, shoes etc. are not allowed. They're also very particular about the values of the students. No cheating, no bullying, etc. (8) Culture. Where do you think your child will be most welcomed? Is your child a SPED student needing special attention? Foreign? Shy? (9) sports (10) leadership (11) extra-curricular cctivities and social development.

Location/ Time.

(1) As much as possible, choose one that is close to your residence, or where you intend to establish a temporary residence. (2) Choose one that won't eat much of your daily time traveling. Anticipate the traffic situation, too. It is kind of stressful for you and your child to travel long hours; otherwise, choose one offering school transport service. (3) If you would ask me, I am not amenable to sending the minor to a dormitory/ boarding house, unless for compelling reasons. There is no safer way to closely monitor your growing children (even those in college) than having them stay with you in the same home.

Budget. Choose one that you can afford based on how much you allocate for your child's education.

Read reviews. Observe. Interview parents or ask for feedback from the students of the school where you intend to enroll your child.

Ocular Inspection. Inquire for admission requirements and set an appointment for a visit on a regular school day and see for yourself how the school operates.

Decide. Wherever you send your child to school, family support is always important to make your child's learning successful and enjoyable.

Important notes:

(1)What is best for one may not be the best for another.

(2) Do not rely solely on the school when it comes to your child's learning. Parents or guardians play a greater role in teaching the child.

(3) Train up the child in the way he should go, and when he is old he will not depart from it (Proverbs 22:6)

Leaving a Progressive Non-Sectarian International School and Transferring to a Traditional Catholic School

After Ezekiel and Zecheriah's egress from MGIS Mahatma Gandhi International School (Manila), we were all floundering whether or not it's prudent to transfer to a local Catholic traditional school, with a purely Department of Education (DepEd) curriculum, effective SY 2015-1016.

As per the latest DepEd bulletin that year, K-12 curriculum is what my children would need in college, leaving us with no other choice but to transfer. Admittedly, the kids' exposure to international education has been superb!

For everyone's guidance and reference, let me share with you what I love most about MGIS: 1)Exclusivity—generally, not more than 15 students per class 2) Individualized teaching, making sure that the students' needs are properly addressed 3)The culture!—Unity in diversity, plus the family atmosphere. Everybody knows everybody 4) Language programs: ESL, Mandarin, Spanish, French, Filipino (PHCL) 5) Students' hands-on exposure to international culture, theater arts, performing arts, music, visual arts and drama; hence, training the students to be versatile 6) and lastly, the sports program covering football, handball, swimming, fencing, archery, basketball, table tennis, chess, taekwondo and a lot more. I hope it remains the same on the years to come. MGIS gave my children a truly international education through its IPC (International Primary Curriculum), and previously International Baccalaureate Primary Years Programme/ Middle Years Programme, and lastly, IGCSE (International General Certificate of Secondary Education) curriculum.

Meanwhile, a lot of parents were messaging me at that time asking where I was planning to transfer the boys. Seriously, I was afraid that they, too, would follow us and I might be charged for "inciting to sedition," hahahah!

We were all aware in the family that the sudden transfer was a trial period. If the boys didn't adjust well, I knew I'd place them back to a good international school.

Now you, too, might have also been intrigued about which school my boys were going to. The new school that I chose was the home of some of our current ecclesiastical leaders in the county and notable political personalities. The students are down-to-earth, street smart, and exhibit laudable leadership skills. As the school is close to a hundred years in existence, it vouches for its possession of a strong combination of traditional and progressive curriculum. They have robotics and the students are well-trained in mathematics and sciences.

Since it's a local school, the tuition fee, including the books and uniform was just around P100,000 (2K USD) which was about 20% of our tuition fee in MGIS. They have many students per class numbering from 30 to 35 students. But a plus, though, was that it's close to our home. The new school was less than one kilometer away from our house.

My boys did well in their one quarter of stay in said local school. They got to easily acclimatize with the new culture and gained new friends in an instant. They also actively participated in academic and co-curricular activities such as the robotics contest, school pageant, filmmaking, and many others.

Just imagine how surprising it was that Zekie and Strong have received academic awards, as well, within the span of their short stay in a traditional Catholic school, with a curriculum that's very different to them! Additionally, Zekie's National Career Assessment Exam (NCAE) taken in the same school yielded 99+ percent rating for academics and non-academics. What a gratified parents Tsip and I were for having produced scholastically brilliant children.

As mentioned, the boys stayed only for one quarter in the local school. Realizing that they needed to have time to develop other skills, they transferred to Victory Christian International School and applied for the homeschool program during the second quarter of the same school year. Through that progressive set-up using Bob Jones American curriculum, the kids got to have opportunities to explore their talents.

Within the span, they attended theater workshops at Repertory Philippines, one-on-one vocal tutorial by celebrity voice coach Annie Quintos-Uy, regular three–days-a-week taekwondo training, driving lessons, playing of drums and keyboard, basic gymnastics, exchange scholarship opportunity to Italy, plus participation in mall shows as hosts and performers.

Anyway, it seems like I can't contain everything within myself those topics I wanted to share in this chapter. There have been more and more stories coming in. To give way to the nitty-gritties of my teaching and lifelong learning experiences, below are miscellaneous anecdotes which I have compiled recently for your guidance and as practical tips:

Classroom Anecdotes by Kumander Misis

Academic Learning from Home

While Strong was reading at home his Heritage Studies book. Topic: Egypt

ME: Go ahead, Strong! Try eating those dry figs brought to us by Aunt Jane from UAE.

STRONG: Oh! Tastes like some kind of a weird raisin, Mom!

ME: Hahah! Egyptians, perhaps, ate them fresh or cooked during those times. Figs are still abundant in Mediterranean coasts, Palestine or in the Middle East. Since we don't grow figs in the Philippines, it's good that you have an idea of what it is.

The Way a Teacher Mom Learns with her Son

I love how my 6th grader son learns world culture and history at home with a balance of secular and Biblical perspective through the Bob Jones curriculum resources. Believe it or not, I have never seen any school book like the one he's using. Again, thanks to the books from BJU Press, USA which are being used in our curriculum at VCIS Victory Christian International School.

In most academic subjects like English, Science, Math and Vocabulary, my sons Zekie and Strong do not even require close monitoring or teaching from me. I would always ask them to approach me for subjects or topics which need clarifications, but they usually do not bother to ask me. Since the curriculum and books are excellently prepared for easy and extensive comprehension. Nevertheless, as a teacher-mom and lifelong learner, it is my choice to read the books with my sons, or independently, before or after my sons do, for personal growth, update, as well as for better appreciation of my sons' curriculum and subjects. It is also quite important to apply in real life through practical approaches the theories found in books. That is exactly, how I get in. By the way, video lectures are also available to back up student's learning (though my sons never used them).

Just like any other profession, teaching has its own ups and downs. And I solidly refuse to be a contributor to the downside of it. These anecdotes are mostly testimonials about my personal classroom experience and encounters, intended to edify and inspire the readers and my fellow international educators:

Teaching makes me even more beautiful

Details: 15 Aug 2013, Mahatma Gandhi International School

Friend: Isn't teaching stressful?

Me: Yes! There are stresses which make you thin, and stresses which make you fat; but, there are stresses which make you even more beautiful. As to the latter...in my case, one of them is teaching!

International Education; Teaching Goals

Date/Setting: MGIS Manila Grade 7 Class, 13 August 2013

It was the first day of SY 2013-2014 where I got into the Grade 7 classroom for my Philippine History, Culture and Language or PHCL class in MGIS.

Everybody seemed excited (since I'm a familiar face maybe) and my intro was: "Congratulations, everyone! Why? Because you're my very first class in MGIS Manila." And there was a big round of applause.

Everyone's energy level was high. We never realized the bell ending our period had rung. I had every student stand up, speak up his mind and exhibit his legible handwriting on the board!

Aside from writing and communication skills, confidence was one of the things I wanted us to develop together. I loved that big class of 16 students including three new comers. It was an active community of French, Pakistani, British, Israeli, Indian, Filipino, Vietnamese, Japanese and Iraqi nationals. Intercultural appreciation and unity in diversity were very much alive!

These kids who are already teenagers today are back to their home countries. Now that they're in their senior high school level, they all remain as friends despite distance. It's only recently that I realized that more than my personal teaching goals for the class four years ago, they have developed a lasting friendship as well.

Teaching Style: Education and Entertainment

Setting: MGIS Manila, 14 Aug 2013 Philippine History Culture and Language (PHCL)

I had only five students in Grade 6. Some of them were still out of the country or on vacation.

ME: Class, let me ask you this million dollar question: "Is PHCL a boring subject?"

STUDENTS: No?! (Uncertain; slow)

ME: Don't worry, your answer will not in any way affect your grades.

Then I asked them the same question for the second time.

ME: Is PHCL a boring subject?

STUDENTS: Ahmm... Sometimes.

Then, we proceeded with the lesson.

Before we wrapped up, I asked the class, again: Is PHCL a boring subject?

STUDENTS (loudly in unison): No!

ME: That's right! There's no boring subject to an animated teacher! There's no boring subject to equally animated students who are ready to learn.

Finally, I asked, "What is a good title for today's session?" Of several choices given by each of them, this title stood out:" Ms. Cherry and her Fantastic 5" . . . And yes, I agreed! They were really fantastic that morning!

As a side note, I also taught PHCL in Grade 5 that same school year. It was an active class of inquirers, communicators, and very helpful ,too! (especially when the Smartboard icons were missing, hahah!) For me, teaching is like running my own tv show. I prepare my program log, divided into timed segments: OBB or opening billboard, 1st segment, 1st gap, 2nd segment (with audience participation), 2nd gap, final segment and CBB or closing billboard. The classroom is a big stage. Teachers are educators and entertainers, as well.

Chapter 22 Journal of a Practical Mom

In celebration of the International Women's Month, I was invited to give an inspirational talk about the "Journey of Motherhood" by a former classmate from the College of Law. As I arrived at the UST auditorium, that classmate twenty-two years ago reminisced with me our school days where as I was studying, I was also a very independent career woman. She said, she never pictured me getting married and having my own family. She added further that I was the least to get to become a mother (as per impression) as I was really busy at the time that she met me.

I have been hearing a lot of stories from friends who had a hard time adjusting from being career women to being full-time homemakers. Actually, being a mom should be a blissful career. And let me reiterate please: "Motherhood is my primary career. All other dealings are just hobbies, sidelines or A.I.D.S (acquired income due to sideline) to sustain my motherhood career.

If only you could adjust, you may also work around the clock, earn as much as you want and enjoy the nice things you were doing when you were still single.

I understand that in the Philippines, we are used to having domestic help doing the laundry, cooking our meals, cleaning our rooms and maintaining our homes. With our busy lifestyle nowadays, however, this routine is no longer worthwhile. First of all, it is a lot of work training your household helper who will eventually leave at her own whim. Secondly, in our case, with long stories to tell, I just don't feel comfortable anymore having a stranger living with us especially on critical years of raising my kids. Now that we have a bigger lawn, I just contract the services of cleaners and a gardener who come to us on weekly schedules to maintain our outdoors.

In my more than a decade of my marriage, I can confidently say how I mastered the art of being a housewife, as well as mom to my two kids, through hands on experience, 24/7. Believing that these lavish experiences may be equally helpful even to single ladies or bachelors, I am sharing some tips with you:

1. Eggs-perience.

Issue #1: My younger boy Zecheriah was such as picky eater when he was younger. His favorite? Egg! But the thing is we cannot give him egg alone all the time as his nutrition will suffer.

Tip: Be very creative. For instance, I cook rolled scrambled eggs or omelettes with spinach or green veggies in it. Another option is that I incorporate boiled chicken eggs or quail eggs on dishes like mixed veggies (chopsuey), burritos, tacos, adobo, stews, menudo, afritada, and so forth. Along the way, I slyly introduced to my kid new flavors with egg as the main attraction.

Issue #2: It takes time to cook fried eggs with all the preparation and waiting. Since I was always on-the-go, I had to double time especially in the morning. Moreover, I wanted to avoid accidental oil spurt or burns specifically when I'm in a hurry.

One alternative I practiced before was to cook my eggs via microwave. Place your egg in a flat microwavable dish, add about a teaspoon of water, beat it and cook for 1.5 minutes. Just leave it and do other stuff (take a bath if you need to) while cooking. Note: Add salt and oil or butter if you want.

2. Microwave and Rice Cooker Cuisine

Rice Cooker Cuisine by Kumander Misis

I can't imagine myself running my home without microwave and rice cooker. For brevity, microwave cuts down my cooking time and adds a lot of convenience on my cookery. Name it! Champorado (chocolate porridge), longaniza (sausages), hotdogs, sweet pork, vegetables, instant noodles, hot water for coffee or tea , hotpot , reheating breads and many more. As to the aspect of whether microwave removes the nutrients on food or whether it is a cause of cancer, that remains debatable. I've been using microwave for twenty years now. By God's grace, I am healthy and well!

When I was the editor of The Manila Bulletin Online, a reader commented:

"I do hope you know the health risks and dangers of using microwaves for food preparation. This might be debatable but there's an exposed radiation using a microwave — and that is obvious.

Using a microwave is so convenient but let's try not to expose our children everyday to microwave 'cuisines' as you've mentioned.

Try to cook the 'eggs' in even if it takes so much time because in the long run, it's more beneficial to our children."

And this was my reply:

Hi!

Thanks very much for taking time in posting your comment. Yeah, I agree that we must "try", as much as possible not to (over)expose our kids and even ourselves to microwaved food. There is, definitely, no substitute in preparing our food the natural way, given the resources and luxury of time. These tips are only "alternatives", based on my day-to-day experience, intended to help out men and women who might be too tied up with work and thinking of simple home solutions such as those suggested.

If I may add, I have been using microwave for 15 years now, and I feel blessed enough that no one in my family ever experienced any negative effects of microwave cooking, so far.

Please feel free to share your thoughts, again, next time.

Sincerely,

Cherry Moriones-Doromal

Editor, Manila Bulletin Online

Rice Cooker Cuisine

Thanks to the wonders of rice cooker, too, where I can cook my favorite pasta, sinigang, nilaga, adobo, tinola, and so on. Today, although I have pressure cooker at home, I also boil my beef for three to four hours via rice cooker. The advantage is that it doesn't require me to look after the boiling process. I feel more relaxed as I generate more time doing other things.

In general, the trick is that you use rice cooker as a multi-purpose boiler or steamer.

Moreover, don't forget to present your food well, it adds to the flavor. Always top your food with fresh herbs to garnish. Most important of all, cook with love!

Chapter 23 Freeze It!

Once more, I would like to give credit to The Manila Bulletin where I published some parts of this article during the time that I was the editor of Manila Bulletin Online.

How exhilarating it is that over the years, despite my innumerable professional adventures, I have retained my online exposure and has transformed my writings into a personal social media ministry, catering on, but not limited to, foodies, social entrepreneurs, families, and housewives. I have more or less around a hundred online accounts comprising of FB pages, blogs, and other social media platforms. Anyway, even then at the Manila Bulletin, I had published practical home and kitchen tips which the readers certainly appreciated. Here's a sample topic that might be of interest to some of you:

In congruence with the extremely hot temperature of our Philippine summer ranging from 40 degrees Celsius and up in the afternoon, here are tips which require cooling down and, in fact, freezing, as well.

To lengthen the shelf life of your food, freeze it! I adopted this practice from a medical doctor friend back in Hollister, California where I stayed for about a month when we were starting our The Phil Am Press operations in Daly City. Her husband was one of my business partners.

To continue with my story, unlike here in the Philippines where convenience stores and food delivery hotlines operate 24 hours a day, in many parts of the U.S., Canada or Europe, these sorts of pampering are not available.

(As a side note, when Zekie was a toddler, I would frequent the United States to explore possible business opportunities there. I would sometimes stay in the US for a month or more. However, seeing via Skype, one day, that my son was turning pale and Tsip was losing weight despite the fact that they have nanny taking care of them the whole time, I rushed back home. From then on, I decided to take care of them and spend most of my time being hands-on with my family.)

In the States, even if the grocery stores, supermarkets or bakeshops were not very accessible especially at night or in the wee hours of the morning, we could eat anything that we wanted because we had frozen victuals. Of course, I'm not referring to raw foods stored in the freezer. I meant ready-to-eat chow like breads, muffins, burgers and leftover cooked Pinoy dishes like sauted mongo, kare-kare (oxtail in peanut sauce), mechado, noodles, and many others. With proper storage and reheating techniques, the taste remained amazingly good as the freshly cooked ones.

When I was experimenting on my The Green Kitchen gourmet products recently, I realized how refrigeration affects the quality and "best before" signals of my homemade artisan food such as my peanut butter crunch. The shelf life which is normally three months is extended up to six months when it's refrigerated.

The shelf life of foodstuff lengthens from one to three months depending on the quality of the food when you cooked or purchased it and how it has been stored, considering the temperature and packaging. Accordingly, we need to package foods correctly to lengthen their storage life. Use airtight containers in the freezer. Cool foods before freezing. Reduce freezer burn by wrapping foods in plastic wrap and seal them in an air-tight zip locked plastic bag.

Save your leftover pandesal for the next two weeks. Freeze it! You have too much adobo for today and would like to have an adobo "baon" next month? Freeze it!

For frozen processed foods like hotdogs, know your lingo. As per experience, I should say that generally, when you see "Best if used by" or "Sell by", it is an estimate for how long the food is expected to retain its flavor, texture and freshness. It is not a safety date. For instance, you don't have to throw out the rest of the milk on the date stamped as "best by". Follow your senses. If it still smells fine, go ahead, you can drink it. However, when you see expiration dates on foods, follow them. Throw out anything in your refrigerator and pantry that is expired. If in doubt, call the customer care hotline of the manufacturer.

Store raw beef, pork, veal and lamb for up to five days in the refrigerator; four to twelve months in the freezer. Poultry and ground meats can be kept in the fridge for up to two days before cooking and up to four months in the freezer.

Also, check the bar code of packaged foods, which is, sometimes, not easy to understand, I know. It may be coded by month, day and year, such as YYMMDD or MMDDYY. Or it may be coded using Julian numbers (365 days), whereby January 1 would be 001 and December 31 would be 365. In even more complex codes, letters A through M (omitting the letter I) are often assigned to the months, with A being January and M being December, plus a numeric day, either preceded or followed by the numeric year.

Last tip before we go. Pour your leftover fruit juice (orange juice, for example) on an ice cube tray and freeze. The next time you make a glass of your favorite fruit juice, (mango, strawberry, etc.) use your "iced juice cube" to make your beverage extra special.

Again, creativity is the key.

Chapter 24 Wow! Eating Manners

Filipinos are known to be food lovers and perhaps, they (we) may be considered as the most flexible ones when we talk about eating.

Colloquially, we call ourselves "cowboys" or down-to-earth—meaning, it's, generally, not a bunch of big deal as to where, what or how we eat, especially in an informal get- together. How we socialize is what is crucial.

You might remember how Former President Erap (Estrada), on several occasions, ate by hand with the masses. President Rodrigo Duterte, on the other hand, would frequently eat simply in his nearby favorite turo-turo in Davao.

It is sometimes mandatory for us to eat by hand for convenience, such as when eating nuts and chips and crabs.

Eating by hand, ladies and gentlemen, means no fork, no spoon, no chopsticks, no utensils.

Military and police officers have the thing called boodle fight wherein rice meal with assorted toppings is served in long banana leaves lined-up on a long table and shared by the whole battalion. There's no plate whatsoever and everybody eats on the same banana leaf. Once more, they eat by hand.

Despite our culture, it is inevitable for us to attend formal occasions and get the chance to see a more convoluted table setting like having three glasses, nine utensils, three plates in front of us. Hence, learning and practicing table etiquette is a must.

In the family, we frequently visit fine dining hotel restaurants as it's a common interest among the four of us. It becomes a bonding moment and sort of reward for ourselves for jobs well-done in school and at work. Additionally, Tsip and I are both sociable. We have gazillions of friends and acquaintances who invite us to dinners and special events. As much as possible, and as a matter of practice, we take our sons with us. The reason is that we wanted to maximize our "we moments" while the kids are not yet busy going out with their own set of friends or attending to other personal matters.

At home, I'm naturally, a sassy girl who loves to leave a fully set 12-seater dining table arranged in my own way complete with plates, bowls, napkins and utensils. As if you're in a hotel restaurant all the time.

Having mentioned that, I used to practically train up my kids to use the right kind of utensils when eating. It's a sort of learning by doing style of training.

To share with everyone these lessons, here's a refresher course. The basic rule in utensils is to start from the outside of your place setting, and work your way toward the main meal plate (service plate). Start with your soup spoon, followed by fish knife and fork, then service knife and fork.

It is often recommended that the salad fork is set to the left of the dinner fork. However, you will encounter formal settings where the dinner fork is placed to the left of the salad fork instead; that is to suggest that the guest looks forward to the main meal before helping himself to the salad.

For cold foods or buffets, let the host announce dinner and wait until the chief guest starts dishing. Sometimes, the host directs the guests as to the manner of approaching the buffet table. For instance, if it is by table number or by wing (guests from left wing or right wing goes to which buffet table), the same is being announced.

Another informative note as culinary experts suggest is that you may start eating hot food when it is served. You do not necessarily have to wait for everyone to begin.

The way to eat:

1. In a buffet set-up. Begin with appetizers, cold cuts, etc. You may skip this part and begin with soup or salad instead if you find it too filling. As a personal tip, what I do is that I discreetly and stylishly nose around all the choices before I decide on which dishes or entrees to

take. I understand that having hundreds of choices may be a perplexing experience.

In the country, we have the thing called "takaw-mata" (voracious eyes) wherein we tend to get too much food beyond what we can normally eat. This is not only a major turn off and obnoxious, it is unhealthful as well. Hence, it is recommended that we do not overload our platter with food. We can always change plate and come back for more.

2. Bread. Before buttering, it is ideal that you break rolls, muffins or slices of bread by hand in half or into bite size. That is break, then butter, break then butter sequence. What I mean is that you do not break the bread into tiny pieces all at the same time and pick them up as if you are eating peanuts.

3. Bacon. If it is crisp, crumble it with a fork and eat with your fingers. If there's fat on it, eat with a knife and fork.

4. Finger foods. If finger meals are offered on a platter, don't put them into your mouth right away. Place them on your plate first. Also, follow the cue of your host.

5. Prawns and Shrimps. In parties, use knife and fork (whenever available) or spoon and fork to take off the head and skin. I know how flavorsome the shrimp head is, but please avoid sucking the head of your shrimps while creating a wild sound and disrupting the other guests.

6. Foods eaten by hand: corn on the cob, spareribs (of course, not the ones in sinigang soup), lobster, clams and oysters on the half shell, chicken wings, chicken lollipops (in informal settings), sandwiches, certain fruits like bananas, olives, celery, dry cakes , veggie strips meant for dipping (eg. carrots,turnips) and cookies.

Just a reminder, by the way, when something gets into your mouth such as an inedible or unpalatable stuff and you want to spew it out, what do you do? For bigger bones other than fish bones and other pieces of food you don't appreciate, the rule is that you covertly spit them into your serviette or napkin, so that you keep the stuff behind the scene.

On the other hand, olive pits must be dropped delicately into your palm before putting them onto your plate. For chicken bones, use your fork to drop them into the plate. Fish bones are meant to be removed with your fingers.

And lastly, as regards the proper way to eat soup in fancy restaurants, it is suggested to scoop the soup from the side of the bowl furthermost from you and sipped from the side of the soup spoon that faces you. Others also suggest that you scoop the soup away from you. Do not bend your head over the bowl; instead, carefully bring the spoon into your mouth to avoid drips. Do not make loud slurping sound. In the Japanese culture, however, slurping sound is intentionally made when you eat your soup as a sign of appreciation. It is unethical for them not to slurp. Chopsticks is used to get the noodles.

Whenever we travel or visit another culture, we may encounter different manners of eating. But, as Filipinos, regardless of where we are in the world, we must never forget our culture of gratefulness. Thank God for the blessings. Thank the host for the invite. And appreciate the waiters or the restaurant manager, or the chef for an excellent service.

I hope I made you smile today as I share these tips.

Chapter 25 The Anti-Stress Science of Facebook

No kidding, writing this article has been stressing me out because I've had a grueling time sorting out which points to include and which to discard.

With our fast-paced millennial world, we have more than enough share of stresses which attack us in all our activities and engagements. In fact, just being alone would sometimes stress us out, too.

Like allergens, germs or viruses, stressors are everywhere. While we can't avoid them, we can deal with them through proper awareness. As to the issue of stress, here with me are four A's on how to deal with it. It is up to you whether to (A1) AVOID the stressor, (A2) ALTER the stressor (A3) ADAPT to the stressor or (A4) ACCEPT the stressor– hence, every time stress would get in the way, I would stop writing and just continue writing on my next available stress-free session.

(A1) AVOID THE STRESSOR

While not all stress can be avoided, you may be surprised, however, by the number of stressors in your life that you can actually eradicate. The first rule, as modern psychologists suggest, is to avoid unnecessary pressures.

Looking at the newsfeed on Facebook gives us an idea on how people of all ages and social statuses react to their daily undertakings. Our Facebook wall, in effect, becomes an open journal free for the public to see.

There was a celebrity who once commented that she never thought everybody wants to be a superstar in his own way, highlighting that everyone on Facebook feels like a pop idol. Oh, well, Facebook statuses say it all. The actress sounded so disgusted by the fact.

Posting shout outs, tweets, blogs or statuses, somehow, allow people to release their emotions.

Do social networking sites like Facebook act as anti-stress formula or, on the contrary, operate as an instant stress factor for you? It is something you have to seriously ask yourself.

Psychologists say stress affects both human brain and body. Consequently, too much of it may have a fatal effect.

It may look as if stress is a lifetime human Siamese twin. The bills keep on coming, business condition is uncertain, work pay is not enough, time chases us as we do errands, demanding career, loathsome personalities, nagging boss, fighting kids every hour or responsibilities you seem cannot fulfill.

Since stress kills, it is imperative that we discover the most effective way for us to manage it. Learn how to organize your thoughts, emotions, schedules and environment. More importantly, polish your skills in coping up with problems.

In doing so, there is no explicit formula. The ultimate goal of stress management is a balanced life– having time for work, leisure, relationships, fun, relaxation, plus the resilience to hold up under pressure and meet challenges face-to-face.

My husband shared with me a very optimistic principle he learned from his police officers' training in Albuquerque, U.S.A. wherein the instructor emphasized the use of the term "situation" as an alternative to the word "problem." Generally, in crisis management, U.S. Police treat the cases only as situations and not problems.

Upon hearing that, I told myself: "That is brilliant!", "that's very me!" Hence, from then on, I would always tell myself, my staff and associates that there is no such thing as a problem, there are only things we call situations. Situations that one can always deal with.

Reflect at how you currently handle stress in your life. Are your coping strategies ideal or unhealthy? Helpful or useless ?

Regrettably, many people cope with stress in ways that compound the problem.

According to studies by psychologists, people these days have come up with their own unhealthy stress coping mechanisms, such as smoking, too much alcohol intake, overeating or undereating, spending hours in front of the television or computer, withdrawing from friends, family, and activities, using pills or drugs to relax, sleeping too much, procrastinating, filling up every minute of the day to avoid facing problems, releasing out stress on others (such as angry outbursts, physical violence).

Guilty or not, one has to realize that while these coping strategies may temporarily reduce stress, they cause more damage in the long run.

(A2) ALTER the stressor (A3) ADAPT to the stressor (A4) ACCEPT the things you cannot change

As said earlier, Facebook seems everybody's most wanted stress journal today. Why not? We are able to socialize, see places, watch movies, view pictures, shop, do business, express emotions and speak our hearts out instantaneously, anytime and anywhere through the charm of FB. Nevertheless, this is not to exempt instances where Facebooking had led to domestic issues. That, of course, is another story.

Facebooking is one way of applying the second A in dealing with stress: (A) ALTER the stressor. Clinical psychologists recommend expressing one's feelings instead of confining them. The principle is that if something or someone is bothering you, it is advisable to communicate your concerns openly. Experts say that if you do not voice your feelings out, resentment will develop and the situation will likely never change at all.

Incidentally, Facebooking is also a means of applying the third A, which is to (A3) ADAPT to the stressor as well as the fourth A which is to ACCEPT the things you cannot change.

Beyond doubt, some sources of stress are inescapable. You can never prevent nor change certain stressors such as the death of a loved one, a serious illness, or an economic downturn.

Do not control the uncontrollable. In such cases, the best strategy to cope with stress is to accept things as they are. But acceptance takes time and process; hence, even if it is difficult, sharing feelings may be very cathartic. The choice is yours. Talk to a trusted friend or make an appointment with a therapist, or write on your FB wall.

Note that if Facebooking or social networking or your methods of coping with stress are not healthful nor helpful, it is time to find healthier ones. The common denominator is that they all require change. You can either change the situation or change your reaction.

Since everyone has a distinct response to stress, there is no sole solution to managing it. When deciding which option to choose, it is practical to think of the four A's I've just mentioned: avoid, alter, adapt, or accept.

Freely experiment with different techniques and strategies. Focus on what makes you feel calm and in control.

The foregoing were derived from researches I made from some published materials of University of Maryland Medical Center, American Psychological Association,Melinda Smith, M.A., Ellen Jaffe-Gill, M.A., and Robert Segal, M.A and other authors. Thus, before I go, let me impart these original tips from me, which may actually be treated as words of wisdom in some degree, whether you are active on Facebook or not:

1. If you want to improve, you must be open for three things:" criticism"","reform" and "transformation".

2. There are things better said than done
And there are things better done than said;
But there are things better said and done
And there are things better not said and not done
Think– that is the whole key, before one says or does anything.

3. There are times when heart and mind bamboozle
It makes decisions even more baffling

While in the past, I believed that when in doubt, one has to follow his heart

As I age and earned life's experiences, now I say, whenever doubt gets in the way ,

> The more you have to scrutinize your heart; hence, mind, in many instances, must prevail.

Speaking of stress and how to manage or avoid it, here's an example of my stressful days or weeks with a quick guide on how to live hassle-free. I regularly post up on social media sites to entertain myself, whenever I find an opportunity.

Attention foreign visitors. Here are some tips for you to demonstrate how life can be this convenient here in the Philippines without housemaid, nanny and driver:

1) Convenience stores all around residential areas are open 24/7; food delivery—from fast food to restaurant food, to home food and healthy meals, local and international cuisine—available as well. What I do in extra busy days is to call the delivery hotlines of my preferred restaurant. Instant meals in a flash.

2) Call laundry service to pick up (wash, press, fold) and deliver your laundry right at your doorstep.

3) In our case, we call the gardener two times a week to clean up the backyard. This is optional, of course. House help available on call, masseuse available on call.

4) Call Grab Express to do an errand for you (buy groceries etc.)

5) Reliable virtual malls and dropshippers are also accessible for quick online shopping.

Today, for example, we've accomplished a lot in just half of our day. And we still look fresh, and ready to party with Miss Universe candidates, hahah!

First, I called Grab Car to pick us up from our home to proceed to Zekie and Strong's photo shoot in school. In five minutes, the Grab arrived and took us to VCIS in Pasig. Wheww! I can't imagine driving from our home in Paranaque to Pasig without stress lines on my face, particularly now that it's summer. From the photo shoot, we booked with the same Grab driver who then took us to Starbucks for to-go breakfast and Peri-Peri for to-go lunch. Next, I got to pay my bills online, talk to clients via Viber and write this post while traversing the road back to our project site

CHAPTER TWENTY-SIX

Avoiding Miscommunication and Missed Communication in our Homes

In an attempt to explain the importance of keeping the home clean, I told my then preschooler son Strong, "Don't make mess or else, ants and cockroaches might eat us. Cockroaches are pests". "Oh, yes, Mom, cockroaches are best", the naive boy replied.

How clear are our messages and instructions? Most conflicts—from a petty quarrel to world war—are brought about by poor communication. Proper communication is the whole key to the success of any relationship, partnership or organization, from one's own home, to the corporate, to a nation.

President Rodrigo Duterte is often misquoted for his comments and public statements. His supporters, especially those who have known him since before his incumbency would always defend him against the media, critics or any attacker. And that is because they have a deeper understanding of the language and manner of speaking by the president. Beyond the words coming out of Tatay Digong's mouth, the keen followers and supporters understand a profounder language, and interpret his words by heart and with empathy based on their previous familiarity about the actions and expressions of the president.

While communication is vital in running a country, it is equally vital in running our own family and in building excellent relationships at home, as well as in our work place, or anywhere we go.

As said earlier, I normally order meals from restaurant delivery hotlines. In doing so, I had experienced many miscommunication issues such as wrong order delivered, order delivered to the wrong address, or specific instructions such as "bring ice", "no pickles", "thigh part requested," were not understood by the delivery hotline representative.

In the family setting, we are aware that every household has its own set of rules, such as come home before 6:00 pm, no grade below 90%, no computer games on weekdays, no boyfriend until 18th birthday, and so forth. The manner of communicating the rules is important, as well.

How do we avoid miscommunication and missed communication at home?

First and foremost, we have to recognize the need to properly communicate with our family. Second of all, make time for communication despite busy itinerary or such other reasons. The following are Kumander Misis' additional tips:

1. ***Express your message, rules or instructions vocally and clearly.***

Parents, don't presume that you are being understood by your kids without even uttering a word. It is unfair to think that what you have in mind is the same as what another person has in mind. For instance, you asked your grade-schooler to study his lessons. The child opened his book and read for five minutes, closed the book afterwards and began playing his tablet. Question: Did your kid study? You'll say "no, he didn't". The answer is "yes, he did".

Irrespective of the briefness of time spent in reading—as in this case, for only five minutes—the child obeyed your instruction. However, it could have been not quite clear to him as to what subjects you wanted him to study and how long you wanted him to read. To make instructions clear, you must give proper and specific instructions. For everyone else, take effort to send text messages or leave notes at conspicuous areas at home, such as: "Reheat before eating", "Feed the dog at 6:00 p.m.", "Get ready. I will pick you up before lunch."

1. ***Clarify your expectations and level your expectations with the capacity of the receiver.***

In communicating with anybody in your family, consider the age as well as the capacity of the person to fulfill your expectations. Be rational. For instance, you are dealing with a senior high student. You may forbid the child from watching movies with friends on a school day, but you cannot totally forbid him from communicating with friends. Socialization is especially active during adolescent years.

1. ***Teach the manner you want your order or instruction to be performed or carried out.***

If you instructed you kid to keep his room clean and orderly, you have to define "clean and orderly". Demonstrate what you mean if possible. For instance, by clean and orderly you mean no unnecessary clutter, well arranged beddings, pillow cases changed every other day, shoes must be put inside the cabinet on the left, etcetera. If you don't do this, chances are, you might get infuriated over and over again for no logical grounds.

1. ***Repeat the message when needed.***

This calls for patience. Do not expect that our children or our wife or husband will understand whatever we want to communicate on the first attempt. It takes unremitting understanding and broad-mindedness for everyone in the family to fortify our relationship.

1. **Be bold to ask questions.**

If there is anything unclear to you, do not be idle nor be afraid to ask questions.

1. **Take time to listen.**

If you're the talker in your home, don't do all the talking all the time. Be sensitive on the feelings of your family members. Listen to what your better half and children have to say. Respect their words and opinions. This is a sure shot for you not to miss any communication.

8. **Speak from the heart.**

An old Filipino adage says: "An honest communication leads to smooth connection". That's right! No pretentions, be transparent.

Communicate. Speak out. Everything that comes from the heart yields power. Remember, while words may be sharp as a sword; silence may be an artful killer.

CHAPTER TWENTY-SEVEN

How Much Does Wisdom Cost?

"In our scholarships, it is God's wisdom not our own that comes into play!"

The other day, I posted about the school fair we went to, wherein representatives from various American universities visited Manila to invite our students or open the possibility for our Filipino students to take college in the US.

Going over the brochures and flyers, for SY 2017-2018, the average school fee for international students in a US school plays around 40-45k USD, or when you are lucky enough to get financial aid or scholarship, the cost would run roughly around 20k-25k USD for a year. By the way, these are public US universities.

Here in the Philippines, the top local private universities will extract some 150k-200k PHP (or 3k-4k USD) out of Momma's pocket a year, whereas school fees for good international schools here in the country run from P500,000 to 2M (10k USD to 40k USD).

That is how expensive education is in our children's generation.

So much about the school fees and all, in my quiet time today, I was led to read the entire Chapters 3 and 4 of Proverbs which give us enlightenment on words "wisdom and understanding".

Proverbs 3: I find Proverbs 3:5-6 quite comforting as it says: "Trust in the Lord with all your heart and lean not on your own understanding. In all your ways acknowledge Him and He will direct your paths."

Looking back at the many years of leaning on God, I just want to repeatedly praise Him for all his favor.

As to the schooling of my sons alone, for instance, Zecheriah "Strong" got accelerated and went straight to Grade 1 in international school MGIS (aside from earning "bragging rights," the same had saved us financially around P300k or 6K USD), next he was given a full scholarship for straight four years amounting to roughly P2M or 40K USD.

God's fountain of wisdom and graciousness did not end up with Strong, as along with it, my older son Ezekiel "Zekie" was also granted a full scholarship amounting to more or less P2.5M (50k USD).

Afterwards, however, due to curriculum changes (K-12) and other factors, I decided to transfer my children to Victory Christian International School where they are currently on Home Study Program using Bob Jones USA curriculum while they are being prepared for real life (undergoing one-on-one special skills training, workshops, and honing of talents outside of the school).

Incidentally, upon entry to VCIS, I was surprised to learn that, again, my boys would be full scholars. And as a bonus, Zekie had another international exchange scholarship opportunity allowing him to explore different schools in Italy last year, 2016. The cost for experience of studying in Europe and meeting people of another culture? Priceless!

By the way, it is mandatory for Zekie to attend a regular school for SY 2017-2018 as he enters his senior high. I am looking at Southville International School or the regular school of Victory Christian International School (VCIS). Let's see.

Who can grasp Your infinite wisdom, Lord?

Our God is bigger than our needs! Our God is bigger than our dreams!

CHAPTER TWENTY- EIGHT

Get Wisdom at Any Cost

"Get Wisdom at Any Cost"—That's the heading of Proverbs 4 (NIV) penned by one of my favorite authors of all time King Solomon. And who, again, is Solomon? Some of you, gentlemen, might say: "Ahhh! I also like Solomon, the king with 700 wives and 300 concubines!" True! But he is also that King of Israel who asked God for wisdom. Having pleased the Lord about his intentions, he was given unsurpassed wisdom, plus wealth and honor. (1 Kings 3:5-13)

If you have time, I suggest that you read the entirety of Proverbs 4. It is concise and beautiful! But for now let's concentrate on verses 7 and 8:

"7 The beginning of wisdom is this: Get wisdom. Though it cost all you have, get understanding.

8 Cherish her, and she will exalt you; embrace her, and she will honor you."

How do we get wisdom?

As a teacher-mom, I am a strong advocate of progressive learning. My kids are very much aware (at least in theory for now, as they're still young) that we get wisdom from combined channels of learning, not only from books. In this family, we make learning as enjoyable and light as possible!

Contrary and with all due respect to traditional learning, we do not set a time limit for learning and teaching in our family. The reason is that every minute is an opportunity to learn. Again, wisdom is not only derived from formal schooling. Whenever we watch the television, we learn from the program, depending on what we watch. When we go to the supermarket, we learn math, economics, promotion, advertising, as well as respect, discipline and patience especially when we have to wait long for our turn in the cashier.

We learn primarily from our family, associates, and mostly from experiences (experiential learning), practice and other avenues such as travel, observation, listening, experimentation, arts, music, sports, socialization and dealing with various people at all levels in society, as well as in service, and engagement in diverse activities which develop our intellect, physique, emotional maturity and discipline.

Above all, we should abide by the ultimate tip about wisdom as contained in Proverbs 9:10: "The fear of the LORD is the beginning of wisdom, and knowledge of the Holy One is understanding."

Though life is a ceaseless learning opportunity for all, and that we learn spectacular things along the way, alone or in collaboration with others, I still believe that those are nothing without fear of the Almighty. For that reason, whatever we learn each day, and through whatever manner, we would like to commit them for the glory of God.

Let me expound a bit on the concept of progressive learning in simple terms. In traditonal school, we learn that 1+1 is 2. In progressive learning, we learn and apply math in practical manners which might have never been discussed in books. For instance, I bought a "buy 1 take 1 apple" from a fruit stand for "pasalubong" to Zekie and Strong. So, how many apples do I have upon reaching home? The books would tell me, 1 apple plus 1 apple equals 2. However, when I opened my shopping bag, I learned that the other apple is rotten and only one is fresh and may be eaten. In reality, my 1+1 apple is not 2 but 1. That is progressive learning. In progressive learning, "real life" situations become our teachers.

As you might have noticed, especially those of you who follow my pages, I write and share a great deal of anecdotes and experiences online, and my posts are found in innumerable sites outside of FB which I, too, can't total. Pardon me as I am constantly excited performing my passion and calling: "To learn, lead, teach, serve, influence and inspire."

Just recently, we have soft-launched "Project Zach", which is basically an art-for-a-cause endeavor. It only started when my now 12-year old son Zecheriah "Strong" Doromal came up with a cartoon character of himself whom he named Zach. Next, we saw the potential of sharing our advocacy on arts with Zach as the spokesperson. Immediately thereafter, we had Zach talk through messages which are being printed on shirts, mugs, caps, paintings and other artwork. Whatever proceeds we get from Project Zach will be utilized in conduct of free art workshops to targeted communities. Anyway, we will tell you more about Project Zach on another book. The main point I'm sharing today is to get wisdom in everything that we do, and share that wisdom to others.

What wisdom have you learned in this life that you can share with others? Each of us is a unique living book where others may obtain wisdom from.

CHAPTER TWENTY- NINE
Adding a Daily Dose of Empathy into my Vocabulary

Every time I am faced with circumstances wherein my patience is challenged, I remember my friend's Facebook post saying that nowadays, patience is no longer a virtue, it's a talent! Last week I took a Grab Car, with Zekie as my chaperone, to meet up with my Mom and finish various business papers afterwards. (Yep, Zekie is too young to get a driver's license). I often prefer riding Grab these days than driving my own car due to the deplorable parking and overall traffic situation around Metro Manila. Furthermore, whenever I take a driver with me on fast-paced days, I feel like I'm carrying an extra child whom I need to attend to.

Anyway, to make the long story short, I opted to take a Grab for convenience, to simplify my life, and to make sure I would arrive at my meetings fresh and stress-free.

Then came this Grab where to our surprise, it was loaded with the driver's entire family—wife, plus two kids—seated at the back of a seemingly unsanitized Avanza. I'm sorry for thinking that the car was dirty because of the trashy interiors with not-so-fresh scent flowing inside the car, plus my seat had bits of cracker residue. To worsen our worst Grab experience, should I share that the daughter kept on barking, I mean "coughing" directly on my left cheek the whole time?!

Honestly, I didn't know how to react. I wanted to cancel my booking straightaway or simply jump out of the car. However, as I looked at the kids and the mother who was wearing either a caregiver's or masseuse's uniform, I broadened my understanding and prayed to God to take control of my temper and to give me enough patience and compassion towards the family who were, perhaps, making time to be together on dad's work.

As usual, the traffic from NAIA to Manila was incredible where I had to bear one hour and twenty minutes of hullabaloo and non-stop coughing from our unanticipated co-passengers.

Question: "How would you feel if you were in my situation?"

It was such an uncomfortable ride for me especially that I am very particular about my health. Please understand that I don't want to get sick or catch viruses as there are also other people relying on me. I would often wear surgical mask in malls and public places despite flu shots, to protect my health, as well as that of my family. Nevertheless, that's beside the point... Believe me, I was talking to myself in silence and kept on chanting internally: "Empathy... empathy... define empathy!"

My being a police officer's wife for the past seventeen years has taught me, and has been teaching me, so much in life. Just like that Grab driver's family, my kids and I would go anywhere Wilson was assigned—Region 4A, Region 3, Metro Manila and even in his Anti-Terrorist Investigation Course in the U.S. It might sound exciting, yet, it's not that easy. It takes a lot of adjustments, quick wise decisions and sacrifices to establish a successful (police officer's) family. As I said before in my previous blogs, one cannot talk to a bird unless he becomes a bird first.

At any rate, I'm just sharing this because I feel so blessed at how the Lord transforms me day by day through various life situations. All I know is that the old me was candid and short-tempered and would not let a seemingly unjust circumstance pass without uttering sarcastic words...I am astounded at my latest discovery.

"Therefore, if anyone is in Christ, he is a new creation: the old has gone, the new is here." 2 Corinthians 5:17

CHAPTER THIRTY

True Life Anecdotes

Fortune in the Midst of Misfortune Part 1

Almost every day, my personal message inbox gets flooded with chain "swerte" or good fortune posts promising the receiver a surprise wealth of fortune on the condition that said post is shared to a certain number of Facebook friends. For instance, "Pass this note to twenty friends and you will receive money in one hour..." and so on.

I don't know whether it's only a cultural thing in the country or also rampant worldwide. People, in general, seem to have a dire thirst for prosperity, and will do whatever it takes to have it.

But here's my confession: "Although I respect everybody else's belief, I'm not an avid fan of those posts and I don't spend a single click to pass chain messages like that." Let me please show you why. Please allow me to leave you two beautiful stories which happened to us in August 2008. I don't know how to make them brief and easy-to-understand by the greater majority, but, here, I'll try.

We were in the U.S. then with our kids, my mom and mother-in-law and were in a van that the then Major Wilson Doromal was driving. Due to the long route that we had to travel to and from Hollister, to San Francisco, to Los Angeles, to Las Vegas and because of the extreme heat in the long dessert, our tire exploded in the freeway as we were traversing the dark freeway back home.

Yes, it was truly dark without trace of a single human in the area. All we were seeing was a vast rice field on both sides of the freeway. I was imagining we were on Elm St. just like what we see in horror movies. We called 911, but we were not even sure where we were as the GPS at that time turned on and off and inaccurate for whatever reason.

Worse, our friends and relatives in that foreign land were all soundly asleep as it was already late.

Who then could help us in such situation? It was difficult because we had two kids on board; and since it was dark, chances are, we might be randomly hit by any vehicle approaching at a high speed.

Would you imagine the then two-year old Zecheriah happened to see a flashlight from somewhere in the car? Then, we got to see the manual telling where the spare tire was, etcetera. A few minutes after, there was a police car patrolling in the area and the police officers came to the rescue.

After which, Tsip introduced himself and shared our concerns with the officers. Then the young police officer of Fresno County himself took effort to change our tire, where he jokingly said, "Wow! It's surprising that Filipino police officers don't even know how to change flat tires!" Then I humorously replied, "Yes, because in the Philippines they have assistants and helpers everywhere." And we all laughed!

On a serious note, I believe in my heart, up to this very moment, that it was our Almighty God who sent those police officers to rescue us. Considering the timing and the overall situation, it was amazing.

In the midst of any troubles, misfortunes, problems or challenges, I hope that we are able to trust that there is a big God who will surely help, sustain, strengthen and bless us. Let us hope, as well, that there be many circumstances and opportunities in our lifetime wherein it is us who will be called to become a channel of help or blessing to others.

Fortune in the Midst of Misforune Part 2

Remember it was in August 2008 that a road mishap occurred to us in Fresno County with my mom? I brought her with us in the U.S. to free up her mind from so much political intrigues at her work in the government. As per observation, I should say that one major downside of working with the government is the tendency to be politically affected by change of administration. In my mom's case, the change of mayor in the city had affected her position compelling her to vacate her post and assume another post, even if she had security of tenure.

With my head up, I can vouch on my parents' integrity. Dad and Mom had lived a simple government employees' life for more than 30 long years since my birth. They used to share their personal resources to bless and serve others and have always been thankful to God for everything. It was through their hard work that they earned their government posts. Upon reaching the age of 65, they retired.

Unlike me who's inherently aggressive and bold and sure to fight when aggrieved, my parents are silent and would constantly leave to God their issues. As regards that, I witnessed how our Lord has His own mighty ways to cheer His people up—such as my parents—and to defend them from those doing them wrong.

Anyway, to continue the story in brief, we went back to the Philippines from the States. Without expectation whatsoever, upon our return, my mom became the lucky and sole winner of a brand new car Volvo S40 at Ace Hardware promo in August 2008. And what's funny was that as far as mom could remember, all she bought was a packaging tape to get to qualify to join the raffle draw. More astoundingly, the year before that, it was also my mom who won the grand prize of another Ace Hardware branch wherein she got a big portable sauna room as prize.

To have won once, it could have been by chance; but, for two consecutive years, and considering the number of branches of participating Ace Hardware stores, there was a clear message being imparted. For that reason, the ACE employees literally kept touching my mom everywhere on her body as well as on her clothes, treating her like a saint, hahaha. "Give us some luck and good fortune, Madam", the employees cheerfully told my mom. While it was how the public interpreted my mom's fate, as to our family, it was the Lord saying: "Keep calm. Relax. (symbolized by the sauna room) Everything is under control. You'll pass through that season. Take a good ride (symbolized by the car). I'm here with you."

Looking from a wider angle, it is clear to me that because of a seemingly inconvenient circumstance experienced by my mother, she got to travel out of the country. Something she wasn't able to do previously as she was so much drenched to work for the past many years. Furthermore, at the same interval, she got to acquire a new condominium unit that became a good investment for her and my dad.

In case you don't understand the point, let me explain that in the Philippines, typical government employees, with their meager salary, can't normally acquire more than one decent property during the span of their service. My parents, by the way, were among those granted by the city government a privilege to own a prime Manila condo unit at a very minimal cost. And lastly, without effort, they got to own a new car out of the blue.

That story demonstrates how faithful and true our God is. His hands are not short for those who put their trust in Him.

If you are currently in a helpless situation, or in a life full of regrets and misfortune, try God. Put your trust in Him, and let His mighty hand perform miracles and wonders in your life.

As we say, while Matthew, Mark, Luke and John had their own Gospel, our personal life is the 5th gospel.

Dear friends, Tales of Kumander Misis is the gospel according to me. And I vow to share more of my stories on my next books, e-books, different forms of media and online channels... all for the glory of God. "May these words of my mouth and this meditation of my heart be pleasing in your sight, Lord, my Rock and my Redeemer." (Psalm 19:14)

Other books by Cherry Moriones Doromal

Tales of Kumander Misis Volume 2

Kodigo Para sa may Asawang Pulis: Sa Kristiyanong Pananaw

Cheat Sheet of a Police Officer's Better Half: Christian Perspective

No Cheating sa Mag-asawang Islam sabi ni Imam

Connect with Cherry Moriones Doromal

https://www.facebook.com/internationaleducator

https://www.facebook.com/kumandermisis/

https://www.facebook.com/brainclips

About the Author

Dr. Cherry Moriones-Doromal is a distinguished Filipina media professional, educator, and strategic communications expert with over 32 years of experience across public relations, quad-media, marketing, and publishing. She currently serves as a host across television, radio, and digital platforms, and was the former entertainment editor and columnist for Republiq Magazine in Southern California.

In 2025, Dr. Doromal was honored as the "Outstanding All-Rounder Woman of the Year" at the 14th World Leaders Summit held at the University of Oxford, UK . She also earned a European Professional Doctorate in Strategic Communication with highest honors, further solidifying her academic and professional credentials.

Her leadership roles have included Editor of Manila Bulletin Online, CEO of Earthwide Concepts Inc. (Las Vegas, NV), and Editor-in-Chief of The Phil Am Press (Daly City, CA). She is also a musical composer, professional writer, and editor.

A licensed educator, Dr. Doromal specializes in English and Literature, with training in International Baccalaureate (IB), International Primary Curriculum (IPC), International General

Certificate of Secondary Education (IGCSE), Multiple Intelligences (MI), and K-12 programs. She holds degrees in Mass Communication, Law, MBA.

Beyond her professional endeavors, she is the founder of "The Green Kitchen," an artisan gourmet brand distributed nationwide through her company, Purple Kitchen Marketing. A portion of the proceeds supports her family's chosen charities. She also launched "Project Zach," a charitable initiative sponsoring art caravans for underserved communities.

Dr. Doromal has been actively involved in the Philippine National Police's transformation programs, serving in various advisory capacities since 2002. Her contributions to community leadership, ecclesiastical work, volunteerism, and social entrepreneurship have earned her numerous awards and recognitions from local government units, the Philippine National Police, and non-governmental organizations.

Her guiding principle, "Born to learn, lead, teach, serve, influence, minister, and inspire," encapsulates her lifelong commitment to excellence and service.

Read more at www.facebook.com/internationaleducator.

www.ingramcontent.com/pod-product-compliance
Lightning Source LLC
LaVergne TN
LVHW090413210926
848480LV00002B/552
9798231289479